Secrets from a Country Kitchen

Secrets from a
Country
Kitchen

LUCY YOUNG

TED SMART

First published in Great Britain in 2004

This edition produced for The Book People Ltd, Hall Wood Avenue,
Haydock, St Helens WA11 9UL

1 3 5 7 9 10 8 6 4 2

First published by Ebury Press
Random House, 20 Vauxhall Bridge Road, London SW1V 2SA

Random House Australia (Pty) Limited
20 Alfred Street, Milsons Point, Sydney, New South Wales 2061, Australia

Random House New Zealand Limited
18 Poland Road, Glenfield, Auckland 10, New Zealand

Random House South Africa (Pty) Limited
Endulini, 5A Jubilee Road, Parktown 2193, South Africa

The Random House Group Limited Reg. No. 954009

www.randomhouse.co.uk

A CIP catalogue record for this book is available from the British Library.

Editor: Susan Fleming
Designer: Roger Hammond at Blue Gum
Photographer: Philip Webb
Illustrations: Madeleine David
Props stylist: Jo Harris
Food stylist: Joss Herd

Papers used by Ebury Press are natural, recyclable products made from
wood grown in sustainable forests.

Printed and bound in Singapore by Tien Wah Press

Contents

Foreword

LUCY YOUNG has worked with me for 14 years and as well as being my 'right arm' is the best friend that anyone could possibly have – day in and day out. Over those years 12,000 people have been to our Aga Workshops – Lucy and I both present the days – and we've written nine cookery books and worked on two BBC TV series together.

Lucy is meticulous in her work and I can get away with nothing. Being the exceptional cook that she is, she has kept my standards very high. I value her opinion, and she's always right – well, nearly always!

Now it is Lucy's turn and here is *Secrets from a Country Kitchen*, full of young, practical recipes, ideas and tips, all with a contemporary country feel. You won't catch Lucy peeling, sieving or blanching unless it is absolutely necessary. Like many of us today, Lucy is coping with a very demanding job, yet still loves having friends round in the evening when she gets home. This means careful pre-planning – often picking up fresh ingredients on the way home from work, then creating a stunning yet simple meal with minimum fuss. In this book she has passed on all her skills and cooking secrets to make home entertaining fun and simple; she explains in detail any tricky stages in recipes, and pays great attention to the final presentation. Everything looks amazing and tastes better than amazing!

No one is more excited or proud than me that Lucy was commissioned to write this book. I know that you will love it and use it. The stickier it gets, the more of a favourite it will be!

Mary Berry.

Introduction

It has been a dream come true to be asked to write my first book. I have been working with Mary Berry for 14 years, running Mary's working life and sharing the teaching at the Aga Workshops (along with a great team). I have also worked on about nine books and two TV series with Mary from her home. Over the years my job has changed enormously. When I first arrived I had a kitchen for testing recipes for books and demonstrations, but my office was literally a cupboard under the stairs (where most people keep their coats), with a shelf for my desk. Now I have a wonderful room fully equipped with a computer and packed filing cabinets! Mary has become my best friend too, and over the years, as the job has grown, we find ourselves thinking the same things and having the same ideas. I have learned so much from her.

Over those 14 years we have also learned a lot from our 'punters', and glean some very interesting stories from experiences in their kitchens. We make mistakes too, for Mary and I are only human, just like you, and we learn from these. For our 'punters', though, this puts their minds at rest. It shows that perfection isn't always the only answer, and that if something goes wrong you can overcome and rectify it.

Secrets from a Country Kitchen is a collection of recipes I have invented over the past few years for family and friends. I felt it was important to go back a little with cooking, not to the absolute basics by any means, but to an understanding of what the important things are when cooking – for we all have such busy lives that simplicity is the key. I am a cook and not a chef, and thus I believe that cooking at home should be hassle-free and not too complicated. Using only the finest ingredients and following the recipe exactly makes it all much easier. I am continually learning from my friends what is important to them when cooking, and hope I have listened and reflected that in my own cooking. None of it should be stressful: although there is a lot of pressure to make a wonderful meal, often simple is best. And ultimately, if you have enjoyed making it, your friends will love eating it.

RECIPES

All the recipes in this book are based on country cooking, devised to appeal to everyone, whether you're cooking for the family or for a dinner party. If you do not live in the country, you can still make them, of course, but I am lucky enough to work from Mary's large, well-equipped kitchen, with a wonderful kitchen garden and herb garden right outside the door. For each recipe I have included how long it takes to prepare and cook, and also whether it can be frozen or not, which I have learned is important to people. I certainly freeze a lot, and have only said it can freeze if it is just as good from frozen as it is when just cooked. I always thaw completely in the fridge before reheating – I wouldn't advise reheating from frozen. Each recipe with a (V) next to it is suitable for vegetarians. Each recipe also has a Tip, which will give you confidence, and many have a Secret. These are the fantastic secrets I have learned during my working life with Mary and show the things that go on in our kitchen – trust me, it can be very eventful!

INGREDIENTS

When devising a recipe, I use only ingredients that can be bought from good supermarkets, local shops or farmers' markets (obviously if you live in the Outer Hebrides, you may not be able to get everything in your local shop!). If I can't buy ingredients from the above, I will not use them; I cannot see the point in having to order an ingredient from a specialised store, putting it in a recipe and then expecting readers to be able to have success. It is also essential to use the very best ingredients you can. If you have a good local butcher or greengrocer, use them. Knowing the source of your ingredients is comforting, and you can ask their advice; their expertise is often second to none.

Using fresh herbs is very important to me, and I rarely use dried ones. You can buy fresh herbs so easily now – or indeed grow them yourself at home. Herbs enhance a dish, so if in a recipe I suggest coriander and you don't like it, replace it with flat-leaf parsley. Don't just leave it out, as the colour and freshness of the herb are very important.

The eggs I use in all the recipes are large, unless stated otherwise.

I am not against using some ingredients from jars or cans: many are of excellent quality. I have given recipes for how to make your own pastry, but supermarkets sell such good ready-made pastries now that I think they are a good idea if time is short.

EQUIPMENT

I believe in making life simple, therefore I don't use a huge amount of specialised equipment. Use a processor if you have one for pastry, and an electric hand whisk or free-standing mixer for whisking egg whites and cake mixtures. I do use cooking rings, which may not qualify as being essential, but they make presentation wonderful – see the Quick Chocolate and Chestnut Mousse on page 160. (But I have also added a Secret suggesting what to do if you haven't got any!) I have used measuring spoons for all measurements; I think they are invaluable in the kitchen as they are so accurate. Weighing ingredients is obviously essential, so you should have a good pair of balance scales. (Digital scales can be temperamental, especially when the battery is running low.)

CONVENTIONAL OVENS AND AGAS

Each recipe has timings for conventional ovens and Agas. Remember all conventional ovens vary. We all get used to our own ovens, and how they behave, and often turning halfway through is all that is needed. Fan-assisted ovens are quicker, and in most recipes the temperature needs reducing by about 20° (but check with your instruction book).

All Agas are different too, and it is a case of learning through experience. When I state in a recipe which set of runners to use, this is counting from the top of the oven. Remember to use a kitchen timer, as it can be a life-saver – with an Aga, you cannot smell if anything is burning!

- Two-oven Agas Roasting oven, top right; simmering oven, bottom right.
- Three-oven Agas Roasting oven, top right; simmering oven, bottom right; baking oven, bottom left.
- Four-oven Aga Roasting oven, top right; baking oven, bottom right; simmering oven, top left; plate-warming oven, bottom left.

Country recipes can be contemporary and easy, as you will see, so I hope you enjoy using this book and will share your results with family and friends. Cooking should be uncomplicated and enjoyable, and I hope I have helped to make your life a little easier, just as pleasurable, and completely delicious!

starters, soups,

nibbles and dips

Red Pepper and Tomato Soup (V) 16
Creamy Celeriac Soup with a Hint of Mustard (V) 17
Healthy Tuscan Bean Soup (V) 19
Individual Asparagus and Quail's Egg Tarts (V) 20
Baked Figs with Parma Ham, Mint and Rocket Salad 23
Quail's Eggs with Hollandaise and Smoked Salmon 24
Fresh Asparagus Milanese 25
Crab and Smoked Salmon Wraps 26
Pan-fried Scallops and Prawns with Rocket 27
Tiger Prawn Filo Bites with Sweet and Sour Sauce 28
My Mate's Mango Salsa Dip (V) 30

Creamy Basil and Tomato Dip (V) 31
Burford Pâté with Cranberries 32
Cheesy Cayenne Biscuits (V) 34
Crostini with Tomato, Basil and Mozzarella (V) 35
Lemon-topped Focaccia Bread with Gruyère Cheese (V) 36
Mediterranean Melba Toasts (V) 38
Midsummer Chutney (V) 39

Red Pepper and Tomato Soup

Ⓥ

This soup, which is perfect for a meal in summer when peppers are so readily available, has a wonderful flavour: it's more pepper than tomato, but very, very tasty. The Boursin makes a change from adding cream, but buy the garlic and herb one, not the pepper one! When whizzing soup in the processor, be careful not to over-fill the bowl and make sure the lid is attached firmly – many an accident has happened, I can assure you!

Serves 4–6 Preparation time 5 minutes: Cooking time 30–40 minutes: Freezes well without the Boursin. Defrost, reheat and whisk in the Boursin to serve

2 tablespoons olive oil
3 red peppers, deseeded and finely chopped
2 large onions, chopped
2 cloves garlic, crushed
1 x 400 g can chopped tomatoes
600 ml (1 pint) Vegetable Stock (see page 184)

1 tablespoon tomato purée
1 teaspoon caster sugar
salt and pepper
75 g (3 oz) Boursin cheese with garlic and herbs, or full-fat cream cheese with garlic and herbs
snipped fresh chives, to garnish

Heat the oil in a large saucepan, add the peppers, onion and garlic, and fry over a high heat for about 2–3 minutes. Add the canned tomatoes, stock, tomato purée and sugar, cover and bring to the boil. Season with salt and pepper, cover, and simmer over a low heat for about 25–30 minutes or until the vegetables are tender.

Remove from the heat and set aside to cool a little. Whizz in a processor until smooth (you may have to do this in batches). Pour the soup into a clean saucepan and return to a low heat. Whisk in the Boursin cheese until there are no lumps of cheese remaining. Check the seasoning. Serve hot with a few snipped fresh chives sprinkled on top.

To cook in the Aga Bring the soup to the boil on the boiling plate, cover, then transfer to the simmering oven for about 30–40 minutes, or until the vegetables are tender.

Tip If you are short on time, use skinned peppers in a jar. I tried both fresh and from the jar when testing this recipe – fresh peppers do have a slightly better flavour, but the ones from the jar are fine too.

Creamy Celeriac Soup with a Hint of Mustard

(V)

Celeriac, with its mild celery flavour, can often be found in country markets, good supermarkets and, occasionally, in vegetable shops. Celeriac is such a versatile vegetable, and so delicious. This is a healthy way to use celeriac – I have purposely added no fat or flour as the potato and celeriac thicken the soup naturally. The mustard here isn't too overpowering, so if you aren't keen on mustard, you may be surprised how much you like this.

Serves 4–6 Preparation time 15 minutes: Cooking time 20 minutes: Freezes well without the parsley

1 large onion, roughly chopped
450 g (1 lb) celeriac, peeled and cut into
2.5 cm (1 in) cubes
450 g (1 lb) potato, peeled and cut into
2.5 cm (1 in) cubes
1.2 litres (2 pints) Vegetable Stock
(see page 184)

450 ml (15 fl oz) semi-skimmed milk
2 tablespoons grainy mustard
salt and pepper
chopped fresh parsley, to garnish

Put the onion, celeriac, potato and stock into a large saucepan. Bring to the boil over a high heat, then cover and simmer for about 15–20 minutes, or until the vegetables are soft and cooked through.

Remove from the heat, and add the milk, mustard and some salt and pepper. Return to the heat and bring to the boil for a couple of minutes, stirring. Set aside to cool a little.

Carefully ladle the hot soup into a processor and whizz until smooth (this will need to be done in batches). Pour back into a clean saucepan and reheat to serve. Check the seasoning, sprinkle with chopped parsley and serve hot.

To cook in the Aga Bring the vegetables and stock to the boil on the boiling plate, cover and transfer to the simmering oven for about 25–30 minutes until tender.

Tip This soup is extremely versatile. It reheats very well (add the parsley at the end to keep it fresh and green) and it can be made up to three days ahead. Celeriac has a very tough, knobbly outer skin, so you will need to peel it with a sharp knife. It would take you weeks with a potato peeler!

Healthy Tuscan Bean Soup

Ⓥ

This wonderful recipe, which hails from the heart of the Italian countryside, is very healthy as it contains no fat or flour. The beans and breadcrumbs help to thicken it naturally.

Serves 4–6 Preparation time 10 minutes: Cooking time 25 minutes: Freezes well without the beans and parsley

1 medium leek, roughly chopped
2 sticks celery, cut into 5 mm (¼ in) dice
1 medium carrot, cut into 5 mm (¼ in) dice
1 x 400 g can chopped tomatoes
900 ml (1½ pints) Vegetable Stock (see page 184)

1 x 400 g can cannellini beans, drained and rinsed
2 tablespoons redcurrant jelly
2 tablespoons tomato purée
4 tablespoons fresh breadcrumbs
salt and pepper
chopped fresh parsley, to garnish

Tip the prepared leek, celery and carrot into a deep saucepan and pour in the chopped tomatoes and stock. Bring to the boil, cover and simmer for about 10 minutes.

Add the rinsed beans, redcurrant jelly and tomato purée, and continue to simmer, covered, for a further 10–15 minutes or until the vegetables are tender.

Add the breadcrumbs and season with salt and pepper. Bring back to the boil over a high heat for a couple of minutes. Garnish with the parsley and serve with warm crusty bread.

To cook in the Aga Cook the leek, celery, carrot, tomatoes and vegetable stock, covered, in the simmering oven for about 10 minutes. Bring to the boil on the boiling plate, then add the remaining ingredients except for the breadcrumbs and parsley. Return, covered, to the simmering oven for a further 10–15 minutes until the vegetables are tender. Add the breadcrumbs, boil for a couple of minutes on the boiling plate, season and serve garnished with parsley.

Tip If you can't get cannellini beans, use butter beans, which are very widely available. Canned beans are excellent – they save soaking dried beans overnight – but be sure to rinse them well. I always like to use Tuscan chopped tomatoes, as they are brighter in colour, and sweeter. Carrots are very easy to grow, but like light or sandy soil the best (they're not keen on clay). Pick quite young, as they are much sweeter to eat.

a secret from our kitchen

We frequently have soup for lunch at work as we often have gluts of vegetables that we need to use up. Soup is fantastic for a large group of people – we make a large batch and freeze what we do not use.

Individual Asparagus and Quail's Egg Tarts

Ⓥ

When asparagus is in season – for a very short time indeed – I always buy it whenever I see it, and use it in a variety of ways. These little tarts are very special, and although they sound difficult, they're really very easy and very impressive too. I've made the tarts with filo as it is the quickest pastry to use: you can buy it fresh or frozen (defrost the latter well). If you prefer to use shortcrust pastry, then of course you can. You can do this recipe leaving out the quail's eggs, but I think it's fun to add them, and they make the tarts very unusual. Don't worry if you break a yolk, at least they look home-made!

Serves 6 Preparation time 10 minutes: Cooking time 25 minutes: Freeze cooked tartlets without the quail's eggs, then defrost thoroughly. Reheat in the preheated oven for about 10 minutes, then crack the eggs into the wells in the tart filling, and return to the oven for a further 4–5 minutes.

9 sheets filo pastry
65 g (2 ½ oz) butter, melted
12 fresh asparagus spears, woody ends
  removed
salt and pepper
175 g (6 oz) Stilton, coarsely grated

2 eggs
450 ml (15 fl oz) double cream
1 teaspoon Dijon mustard
1 tablespoon snipped fresh chives
12 fresh quail's eggs

Preheat the oven to 200°C/400°F/Gas 6, and preheat a flat baking sheet too. Grease a 12-hole muffin tin with a little of the melted butter.

First make the filo cases. Brush each sheet of filo with melted butter and cut each sheet into four. Arrange three of these little squares on top of each other in a star shape. Push each pile into each muffin hole (some filo will stick up over the top, this is fine).

Cut the tip off each asparagus spear (about 4 cm/1½ in long), and cut the stalks into 1 cm (½ in) pieces. Cook the stalks in boiling salted water for about 1 minute, then add the tips for a further minute. Drain and refresh in cold water until stone cold, then dry in a tea-towel. Put the tips to one side, and divide the stalks between each pastry case. Divide the Stilton equally between the tartlets on top of the asparagus stalks.

Whisk the eggs, cream, mustard and chives together in a bowl until smooth, and season with a little salt and pepper. Pour equally between the cases. Top with the asparagus tips. Carefully transfer to the preheated oven and the hot baking sheet and bake for about 15–20 minutes or until the filling is just set and the

continued next page

pastry is turning golden brown. Carefully remove from the oven.

Make a slight well in the centre of each tart, using the back of a teaspoon. Crack a quail's egg into each well (the egg will sit on top of the tart). Return to the oven for a further 4–5 minutes until the egg white has set and yolk is still just runny. Serve warm with dressed salad leaves.

To cook in the Aga Slide the muffin tin on to the grid shelf on the floor of the roasting oven for about 10 minutes. Remove the grid shelf and place the tin directly on the floor of the oven for a further 7–10 minutes, until the pastry is cooked underneath. Crack a quail's egg on top (as described above) and return to the floor of the roasting oven for a further 4–5 minutes.

Tip When using filo, be sure to keep it wrapped in clingfilm or a damp tea-towel as it can dry out very quickly. Our kitchen has an Aga, which makes the kitchen particularly hot and drying for filo.

Baked Figs with Parma Ham, Mint and Rocket Salad

This is such an unusual starter, and it's delicious even if you're not mad about figs! It's also wonderful served with a cheeseboard at the end of a meal. Fig trees grow very happily in most country (and town) gardens, and even in pots (they do get very large, so will need transferring at some stage). At home I have a lovely fig tree, which I prune back well so that it produces figs throughout the summer. Pick as soon as ripe, as they turn mushy if left for longer, and the birds will probably get there before you! Fig leaves are lovely for garnishing a platter.

Serves 4 Preparation time 5–10 minutes: Cooking time 15 minutes: Not suitable for freezing

4 small fresh figs, halved lengthways
   through the stalk
a little runny honey
2 tablespoons chopped fresh mint
50 g (2 oz) Dolcelatte cheese, coarsely
   grated

black pepper
1 x 50 g bag fresh rocket
a little salad dressing (see secret)
4 slices Parma ham

Preheat the oven to 200°C/400°F/Gas 6.

Arrange the figs snugly, cut-side up, in a small ovenproof dish. Brush the cut side of each fig with a little runny honey, then sprinkle over the chopped mint.

Top each fig with the Dolcelatte and season with black pepper. Bake in the preheated oven for about 15–20 minutes, or until soft and golden brown.

Divide the rocket between four plates, and pour over a little salad dressing. Arrange one slice of Parma ham on top of the rocket leaves. Arrange two fig halves on top of the ham and serve at once with crusty bread.

To cook in the Aga Slide the dish on to the top set of runners in the roasting oven for about 15 minutes until soft and golden brown.

Tip Parma ham (*Prosciutto di Parma*) is Italian dry cured ham. You can use Black Forest or Serrano ham if you prefer. You can prepare these in their dish up to 12 hours ahead.

Quail's Eggs with Hollandaise and Smoked Salmon

This is a stunning canapé and so easy to do. Arranged on a large platter and garnished with fresh herbs, it's perfect for a wedding or special occasion.

Makes 24 canapés Preparation time 10 minutes: Not suitable for freezing

12 quail's eggs
celery salt
a little good-quality hollandaise sauce
   from a jar

1 large slice smoked salmon, cut into
   24 small pieces
24 tiny sprigs fresh dill
black pepper

Cover the quail's eggs with cold water in a saucepan, bring up to the boil and, once the water is boiling, boil for 3 minutes. Drain and cool under running cold water.

Peel the eggs, cut in half lengthways, and lay cut-side up on a platter. Sprinkle each cut side with a good pinch of celery salt. Spoon a tiny (sultana size) amount of hollandaise sauce over the egg yolk.

Arrange a piece of smoked salmon on top of the hollandaise and garnish with a sprig of fresh dill. Sprinkle with a little coarsely ground black pepper. Serve at room temperature.

Tip Quail's eggs can be tricky to peel, so once they are boiled and cold, peel immediately – it's much easier when they are freshly cooked. They will keep, peeled, in a plastic bag in the fridge for a few days. The canapés can be made up to 12 hours ahead, carefully covered in clingfilm, and kept in the fridge.

Fresh Asparagus Milanese

Asparagus is a one of my favourite first courses, and this recipe is one you can prepare ahead (but don't be tempted to overcook the asparagus). It reminds me of my favourite Italian restaurant in the lovely riverside town of Marlow, where I always order asparagus with Parmesan. The atmosphere is second to none, and for any family birthday celebration, we end up there. It's a very noisy restaurant, so perfect for my immediate family – there are nine of us!

Serves 4 Preparation time 6 minutes: Cooking time 5 minutes: Not suitable for freezing

24 fresh asparagus spears
salt and pepper
4 slices Parma, Black Forest or
   Serrano ham

25 g (1 oz) Parmesan shavings
a little balsamic vinegar or a good bought
   hollandaise sauce

a secret from our kitchen

Always buy fresh Parmesan in a block. It is so much better than the ready-grated Parmesan in a tub that you buy from supermarkets. Keep Parmesan in a paper bag in the fridge, not in clingfilm, otherwise it will sweat and go mouldy quickly.

Cut the woody stalks from the ends of the asparagus spears. Using a potato peeler, pare 5 cm (2 in) off the bottom, removing the tough skin. Add the asparagus to a pan of boiling salted water, and boil for about 4 minutes until just tender. Drain, then refresh in cold water until stone cold. Dry on kitchen paper.

Bunch together six asparagus spears in four bundles. Wrap a piece of Parma ham round the base of each bundle. Arrange on an ovenproof plate (preferably one with no sides), and season with pepper. Divide the Parmesan between each bundle on top of the Parma ham. Cover with clingfilm and chill until ready to serve.

Preheat the grill.

Place the plate of asparagus bundles under the hot grill for about 3–4 minutes until the cheese has melted and the asparagus is piping hot. Drizzle over a little balsamic vinegar or add a dollop of hollandaise sauce. Serve immediately with crusty bread.

To cook in the Aga Slide the ovenproof dish on to the top set of runners in the roasting oven for about 5 minutes until piping hot.

Tip Do choose your fresh asparagus carefully: dark green spears have the best flavour, as the pale variety can be a bit tasteless. The English asparagus season is between May and July.

Crab and Smoked Salmon Wraps

When you are in the country, somewhere like Norfolk or Devon, say, you can buy fresh crabs from the fishermen or local shops. Buy them dressed, or buy them live and cook them yourself at home. I often go 'crabbing' with my nieces and nephews in Salcombe in Devon – the kids love it and it is so easy to do. The best way of catching crabs is to use raw bacon as bait. One day we only had Parma ham – I thought the crabs would never know the difference but we caught none and were the laughing stock on the quay! I have used canned crab meat for this recipe, which I think is very good, but be sure to drain it very well. These wraps make a quick and easy cold first course, and they can be prepared ahead. They're ideal for a large dinner party, and look very pretty too.

Serves 4 Preparation time 15 minutes: Not suitable for freezing

50 g (2 oz) full-fat cream cheese
2 tablespoons low-calorie mayonnaise
2 tablespoons chopped fresh dill
1 tablespoon lemon juice
1 x 175 g can white crab meat, drained
1 egg, hard-boiled and roughly chopped
8 cocktail slices smoked salmon
salt and pepper

To serve
lamb's lettuce
a little salad dressing
1 lemon, quartered

Mix all the ingredients together in a bowl, except for the smoked salmon, seasoning to taste with salt and pepper.

Lay the smoked salmon slices out on a board and season with black pepper. Divide the mixture into eight and spoon one portion at one end of each strip of smoked salmon. Tightly roll the smoked salmon up to form a fat cigar shape.

Arrange the lamb's lettuce on individual plates and dress with a little salad dressing. Arrange two salmon parcels on each plate – one standing upright and one lying down – and garnish with a wedge of lemon.

Tip Cocktail slices of smoked salmon are long and thin and perfect for this recipe. If you cannot find them, cut long thin strips from any smoked salmon you buy. And if you have any trimmings left over, you can chop them and add them to the filling.

a secret from our kitchen

There are more than 4500 types of crab that vary in size and colour. The brown crab is the most common to our shores and the most widely available to buy. If catching your own crabs or buying them live, be sure to choose the heaviest you can – the weight shows the crab is fully grown inside the shell and is full of meat. After cooking, insert the tip of a knife round the edge of the shell to open it. There are two sorts of meat: the soft rich dark meat inside the upper shell and the white meat in the claws and body. Be sure to remove the gills under the belly as these are unsafe to eat.

Pan-fried Scallops and Prawns with Rocket

This is a fresh starter, which takes seconds to cook – a more up-to-date version of garlic prawns, with a deep flavoured glaze. Be careful not to overcook the prawns and scallops or they will become rubbery. This recipe is very quick: weigh it out ahead and just fry at the last minute. If you or your guests are not keen on scallops, then replace them with eight more prawns.

Serves 4 Preparation time 5 minutes: Cooking time 5 minutes: Not suitable for freezing

1 x 50 g bag wild rocket
1 tablespoon olive oil
12 shelled king scallops, with coral
12 raw tiger prawns, shells removed
1 large clove garlic, crushed
1 x 2.5 cm (1 in) piece fresh root ginger,
   peeled and finely grated

juice of 1 lemon
2 tablespoons soy sauce
1 tablespoon runny honey
a few sesame seeds

Divide the rocket between four plates.

Heat the oil in a non-stick frying pan over a high heat. Add the scallops and cook for about 30 seconds. Add the prawns, and once they have turned pink on one side, turn them and the scallops over and cook for a little longer until the prawns are pink all over and the scallops are just cooked. Transfer to a plate.

Add the remaining ingredients to the pan (except for the sesame seeds), with 2 tablespoons water. Continue to fry over a high heat so that the sauce reduces to a thick glaze. Return the seafood to the pan and toss so that it is all coated in the glaze.

Arrange three scallops and three prawns on the top of each pile of rocket, and pour over the caramelised sauce. Sprinkle over a few sesame seeds and serve immediately.

To cook in the Aga Cook in a frying pan on the boiling plate.

Tip King scallops are larger than queen scallops and, I think, have more flavour, but you can use either. Serve the corals with the scallops, as they add lovely colour and give a different texture.

a secret from our kitchen

Rocket can often be quite tricky to grow at home, especially if your garden has flea beetles. The beetle loves rocket and leaves tiny holes in the leaves, which are not pretty in a salad! Most of the damage is done in April and May when the weather is dry, but covering seedlings with fleece in the first couple of weeks of germination can help to limit the damage. Georgie and Stu, great friends of mine who live in London, have rocket growing freely in their garden. I think their soil must be blessed as there is not a hole in sight!

Tiger Prawn Filo Bites
with Sweet and Sour Sauce

These prawns are perfect for serving at a party, as they look impressive and are very easy to do. I have left them plain because the sauce has a wonderful depth of flavour – but you really do need to serve the sauce with the prawns. The sauce can be used with many other recipes.

Makes 15 bites Preparation time 10 minutes: Cooking time 10 minutes: If the prawns have not been frozen before, freeze wrapped raw filos. Defrost in the fridge and cook as below

2 sheets filo pastry
50 g (2 oz) butter, melted
salt and pepper
15 (about 225 g/8 oz) raw tiger prawns, shelled but with tails left on

Sweet and sour sauce
2 tablespoons sweet chilli dipping sauce from a jar
4 tablespoons rice wine or white wine vinegar
4 tablespoons dark muscovado sugar
2 tablespoons water

First make the sauce. Measure all the ingredients into a small saucepan. Bring to the boil, stirring until the sugar has dissolved, then pour into a small container to cool.

Preheat the oven to 200°C/400°F/Gas 6.

Brush each sheet of filo with melted butter. Put one sheet on top of the other, and season with salt and pepper. Using a sharp knife cut the filo in three lengthways, then cut five strips widthways so you have 15 double squares.

Put one prawn in each square. Pull the prawn slightly so it becomes straighter, and wrap the filo around the prawn so only the tail is showing. Transfer to a greased baking sheet or a baking sheet lined with non-stick paper. Brush the filo prawns with a little more melted butter, and bake in the preheated oven for about 10 minutes, turning halfway through, until the pastry is golden brown and crisp, and the prawns are cooked.

Serve while hot with the cold sweet and sour sauce.

To cook in the Aga Slide the baking sheet on to the floor of the roasting oven and bake for about 8–10 minutes, turning halfway through cooking time.

Tip North Atlantic or large tiger prawns are perfect for this recipe. The longer and thinner they are, the better. The round curled-up ones do not look so good.

My Mate's Mango Salsa Dip

I first had this salsa at a great friend's house – it really is delicious, so thank you, Lou, for this recipe. Serve as a dip in a bowl or as a side sauce with grilled or baked fish. It is important to cut all the ingredients very small for this recipe – the chopped pieces should be about the size of a raisin.

Serves 4–6 Preparation time 10 minutes: Not suitable for freezing

1 medium ripe mango
1 small green chilli
1/2 small red onion
4 tomatoes
2 tablespoons coarsely chopped fresh
  coriander

Dressing
3 tablespoons olive oil
1 tablespoon lemon juice
  salt and pepper

Cut into the mango on either side of the large flat stone, cutting off two fat ovals of skin and flesh. Peel and cut the flesh into very small cubes, not forgetting the flesh still attached to the stone. Tip into a bowl. Cut the chilli in half, discard the seeds, chop the flesh very finely and add to the mango. Halve the onion again, and cut into very thin slices. Cut the tomatoes in half, remove the seeds, and cut the flesh into small cubes the size of the mango. Add the tomato and onion to the bowl.

Mix the dressing ingredients together, stir into the bowl, and season with salt and pepper. Chill, covered in clingfilm, before serving.

Serve as a dip with Doritos, toasted pitta breads or tortilla chips.

Tip Green chillies are milder than red ones, so if you want it really hot, add a red one instead. The smaller the chilli, the hotter it is. The seeds from a chilli are the hottest part, so be careful not to get them near your eyes. And always wash your hands well after handling chillies.

Creamy Basil and Tomato Dip ⓥ

This dip is perfect as a starter for a casual party, or for a buffet table. Anything can be dipped into it – pitta bread, bread sticks or potato wedges. This dip is also very good in a jacket potato instead of butter, or in a sandwich instead of mayonnaise.

Serves 4–6 Preparation time 5 minutes: Not suitable for freezing

1 x 200 g tub Greek yoghurt

3 tablespoons low-calorie mayonnaise

a large bunch of fresh basil

4 tablespoons sun-dried tomato paste

2 tablespoons mango chutney

1 teaspoon lemon juice

Measure all the ingredients into a processor and whizz until just smooth. Taste and check for seasoning.

This can also be done by hand. Tear the basil into small pieces and mix with the other ingredients.

Tip A bonus of this dip is that it can be made up to two days ahead – the flavours will improve with time.

a secret from our kitchen

If you have bought a pot of basil from the supermarket, keep it on the windowsill, don't put it in the fridge: it is a Mediterranean herb, so is used to a warm climate. Do be aware that the stems are weak and straggly because growers force the baby shoots (so that supermarket shelves are always full). As soon as you take the plastic off, the stems will fall over unless you support them with skewers or bamboo canes and tie up. This will actually encourage strength in the stems, and new shoots to grow.

Burford Pâté with Cranberries

I devised this smooth pâté recipe when I was going away with friends for the weekend. Burford, in the Cotswolds, is such a pretty village with its distinctive oolitic limestone shops and houses. There are very nice pubs, too! My preference is for smooth pâté, served with chutney, so in this recipe I have added the cranberries to give a little fruitiness.

Serves 4–6 Preparation and cooking time 10 minutes: Not suitable for freezing

If you wish to make
the pâté and serve
it in a terrine, but
don't have a smart
china one, put it in a
metal terrine or loaf
tin lined with
greaseproof paper or
clingfilm. Turn out,
remove the paper or
clingfilm, and
garnish with sprigs
of thyme as above.
If using a china
terrine, I think it is
nicest to serve it
from the terrine.

100 g (4 oz) smoked streaky bacon, snipped into pieces

1 small onion, finely chopped

1 clove garlic, crushed

2 tablespoons sunflower oil

450 g (1 lb) chicken livers, trimmed

100 g (4 oz) butter, softened

225 g (8 oz) full-fat cream cheese

6 cream crackers, broken into pieces

2 tablespoons each of chopped fresh sage and thyme

2 tablespoons lemon juice

75 g (3 oz) dried cranberries

salt and pepper

sprigs of fresh thyme, to garnish

Heat a large non-stick frying pan over a high heat, add the bacon and allow the natural fat to come out. Add the onion and garlic and fry for a few minutes. Reduce the heat, cover and simmer for about 15 minutes until the onion and bacon are cooked. Using a slotted spoon, transfer the contents of the pan to a plate, and leave to cool.

Add the oil to the same pan along with the chicken livers, and cook over a high heat for 2–3 minutes on each side until cooked through. Set aside to cool.

Measure all the remaining ingredients, except for the cranberries, into a food processor. Add the cold bacon, onion and chicken livers and whizz for a few minutes until completely smooth. Add the cranberries and whizz for a few more seconds so the cranberries are still chunky. Add a little salt and pepper to taste.

Spoon the pâté into a terrine or six ramekins, cover with clingfilm and transfer to the fridge to firm up a little.

Garnish with sprigs of thyme and serve at room temperature with Melba toast (see page 38) or normal toast.

To cook in the Aga Cook the bacon, onion and garlic in a frying pan on the boiling plate for a minute, cover and transfer to the simmering oven for about 20 minutes until tender. Return to the boiling plate to drive off any wetness. Brown the livers in a frying pan on the boiling plate.

ⓥ Cheesy Cayenne Biscuits

These crunchy biscuits are perfect with drinks before dinner or with cheese after lunch or dinner. They can be made and popped in the freezer until you need them. The cayenne pepper gives a little kick but won't make the biscuits too hot. There may not seem to be a large amount of Rice Krispies, but trust me, they make all the difference to the recipe.

Makes 42 biscuits Preparation time 10 minutes: Baking time 20 minutes: Freezes well

100 g (4 oz) plain flour
50 g (2 oz) mature Cheddar cheese, grated
75 g (3 oz) butter, softened
1/2 teaspoon baking powder

1/4 teaspoon cayenne pepper
15 g (1/2 oz) Rice Krispies
salt and pepper

a secret from our kitchen

These biscuits keep well in a plastic box in the fridge, layered with kitchen paper. We like to refresh our biscuits in a moderate oven for about 5 minutes before serving, as this crisps them up a little if they have been frozen or kept in the fridge.

Preheat the oven to 180°C/350°F/Gas 4.

Measure all the ingredients, except the Rice Krispies, into a food processor. Season with salt and pepper and whizz until the mixture forms a ball (you can mix by hand in a large bowl if preferred). Turn the dough into a bowl and mix in the Rice Krispies with your hands.

Shape into balls the size of small walnuts, and arrange on a greased baking sheet. Using your fingers, press the balls down a little so they are slightly flat and more like a thick pound coin.

Bake in the preheated oven for about 20 minutes until lightly brown all over. Transfer to a wire rack to cool.

To cook in the Aga Slide the baking sheet on to the grid shelf on the floor of the roasting oven for about 10–12 minutes until golden brown. Slide in the cold sheet on the second set of runners after about 5 minutes if getting too brown.

Tip Do not worry about spacing the raw biscuits out too much on the baking sheet. The baking powder helps them to rise a little and keep their shape, preventing them from spreading too much. Try to keep them fairly small – they should be bite-sized.

Crostini with Tomato, Basil and Mozzarella

Ⓥ

In the summer I always have a pot of basil in the window or – if it's really hot – outside the back door. I use it all the time. These crostini are delicious bites, that can be popped under the grill at the last minute. They are very user-friendly, for once they are made untopped, you can use any topping you like. You can also serve three of these as a starter.

Makes 20 crostini Preparation time 5 minutes: Cooking time 10 minutes: The crostini alone freeze well just toasted

1 thin baguette, cut into slices about 1 cm (½ in) thick
olive oil
green pesto from a jar

3 large tomatoes
100 g (4 oz) mozzarella cheese, sliced
salt and pepper
fresh basil leaves

Preheat the grill.

Brush the sliced bread on one side with the oil. Place on a baking sheet, oil side up.

Slide under the grill and toast for 3–4 minutes until golden brown. Remove from the oven, turn the bread over and spread with a little pesto.

Cut the tomatoes in quarters, remove the seeds and slice lengthways fairly thinly. Arrange a couple of tomato slices and a little mozzarella on top of the crostini, and season with salt and pepper. Return to the grill for about 5 minutes until the cheese has melted and browned a little.

Top each crostini with a basil leaf, and serve warm.

To cook in the Aga Slide the baking sheet on to the floor of the roasting oven and bake the crostini for about 3–4 minutes on each side until golden brown. Continue as above for the topping, then return to the top set of runners in the roasting oven for about 5 minutes until the cheese has melted and browned a little.

Tip Crostini freeze fantastically, without the topping. If making ahead, just oil the bread slices on each side then grill until golden brown. Freeze in a plastic box layered with kitchen paper. Large basil leaves are best torn with your hands. Chopping them with a knife can bruise the leaves and turn them black.

Lemon-topped Focaccia
Bread with Gruyère Cheese

(V)

Focaccia bread is a staple of Italian country cooking, and you can buy it everywhere these days. I think, however, that making your own bread is really fun and rewarding to do. Focaccia is the easiest of breads to make, as the rising time is quite short compared to other breads. Serve it warm or cold, cut into chunks, with a bowl of olive oil and balsamic vinegar to dip into. A great starter for a relaxed lunch.

a secret from our kitchen

If you haven't a mixer or processor, mixing and kneading by hand can be quite therapeutic! You may find it difficult to find a plastic bag big enough for the dough and baking sheet – to solve this problem we often use a brand new, clean, white bin liner.

Serves 6–8 Preparation time about 2 hours, including rising and proving time: Cooking time about 25 minutes: Freezes well

500 g (1 lb 2 oz) strong white flour
1 x 7 g packet dried yeast
1 tablespoon salt
4 tablespoons olive oil
350 ml (12 fl oz) warm water

Filling and topping
175 g (6 oz) Gruyère cheese, grated
2 tablespoons chopped fresh parsley
4 tablespoons olive oil
4 cloves garlic, crushed
finely grated zest and juice of 1 lemon

Preheat the oven to 220°C/425°F/Gas 7.

Measure the dough ingredients into a free-standing mixer or processor, and mix together until you have a sticky, soft dough. Lift the dough on to a floured work surface and knead by hand for a few minutes. Transfer to an oiled bowl, cover with clingfilm and leave to rise in a warm place for about an hour or until doubled in size.

Tip the dough out of the bowl on to a floured work surface and knock back by hand (you may need to flour your hands to do this). Roll the dough out using a rolling pin to about 30 x 40 cm (12 x 16 in). Sprinkle the cheese and parsley over one-half of the dough, fold over the other half and re-roll back to the same size. Slide on to a baking sheet. Using your fingers, make ten large holes evenly across the surface of the dough.

Mix the oil, garlic and lemon zest and juice together in a small bowl and pour over the top of the bread. Slide the dough and baking sheet into a large plastic bag and leave in a warm place to prove for about 30 minutes or until it has doubled in size.

Remove the baking sheet from the bag and slide into the preheated oven, near the top. Bake for about 20–25 minutes or until golden brown both on top and underneath, and sounds hollow when the base is tapped. Serve warm, or leave to cool.

To cook in the Aga For the rising, sit the bowl at the back of the Aga, and do the same for the proving on the baking sheet (this is the perfect place). To bake, slide the baking sheet on to the floor of the roasting oven for about 25 minutes. After 15 minutes, slide the cold sheet on to the second set of runners if the bread is getting too brown. Cook until golden brown on top and underneath, and the bread sounds hollow when the base is tapped.

Tip Do be sure to allow time for the dough to double in size when rising and proving, as this makes all the difference to the finished bread, giving a light texture, not a heavy dense one. Try not to include too much extra flour when kneading, as this will make a dry dough.

Mediterranean Melba Toasts

(V)

This is such a quick and easy nibble to go with drinks before a meal. You can use different flavourings if liked: tapenade or pesto, for instance, would be just as delicious.

Makes 24 bites Preparation and cooking time 15 minutes: Plain toasts freeze well

3 medium slices white bread	finely grated Parmesan cheese
sun-dried tomato paste from a jar	12 pitted olives, cut in half

Preheat the oven to 180°C/350°F/Gas 4.

Toast the bread in the usual way. Remove the crusts and cut through each slice horizontally. Remove any excess dough from the centre. (To make plain Melba toasts, simply toast the untoasted sides now – being careful, they burn easily.)

Spread each untoasted side with a thin layer of sun-dried tomato paste. Cut each half of toast into four diagonally. Sprinkle each triangle with Parmesan cheese and place an olive half in the centre.

Transfer to a baking sheet, and bake in the preheated oven for about 5 minutes until hot and slightly crisp and the edges curl up. Serve warm.

To cook in the Aga Slide the baking sheet on to the floor of the roasting oven for about 5 minutes until hot and crisp, or cook in the simmering oven for about 25 minutes until hot and the edges curl up.

Tip Melba toast triangles (without topping) can be frozen in a plastic box, or will keep for a few days in an airtight container or plastic bag in the larder. Parmesan cheese comes from northern Italy. Authentic Parmesan comes in huge drum shapes, which are stamped all round with the words 'Parmigiano Reggiano'. This guarantees its origin.

Midsummer Chutney

Ⓥ

Make chutneys on a day when you can open windows, as the smell of vinegar is very strong! In the Aga at work it is especially easy to make, as chutney is cooked in the simmering oven so there aren't too many vinegar fumes in the kitchen. I think a jar of home-made chutney makes a lovely present if going out for dinner, instead of chocolates or flowers. If the jars are sealed well, a chutney will be even more delicious a few months after making as the flavour matures.

Makes 1.3 kg (3 lb) Preparation time 15 minutes: Cooking time 1 hour: Not suitable for freezing

450 g (1 lb) onions, roughly chopped

450 g (1 lb) (2 small) aubergines, chopped into 5 mm (¹/₄ in) cubes, skin on

450 g (1 lb) courgettes, cut into 5 mm (¹/₄in) cubes, skin on

3 x 400 g cans chopped tomatoes

2 red peppers, deseeded and cut into 5 mm (¹/₄ in) cubes, skin on

1 tablespoon salt

1 tablespoon ground cumin

a good pinch of hot chilli powder

2 teaspoons ground allspice

300 ml (10 fl oz) white wine vinegar

450 g (1 lb) granulated sugar

Tip the onions, aubergines, courgettes and canned tomatoes into a large saucepan. Bring to the boil, cover with a lid, and simmer over a low heat for 30–40 minutes or until the vegetables are very soft.

Add the remaining ingredients, stir until the sugar has dissolved, then reduce over a high heat for about 15 minutes until you have a thick chutney consistency and there is no surplus liquid.

Spoon into sterilised jars (see below) and seal.

To cook in the Aga Cook the first stage, covered, in the simmering oven for about 40 minutes. Remove the lid, add the other ingredients, and boil on the boiling plate for a further 10 minutes until a thick chutney consistency.

Tip To sterilise the jars, pour boiling water inside and pour out again, or put through a cycle of the dishwasher. Ensure the lids fit properly to prevent any mould forming. The secret of a good chutney is to reduce the liquid – don't bottle when too wet.

a secret from our kitchen

I think that chutney is great fun to make, especially when you have plenty of home grown vegetables. Even if you don't, there are so many vegetables to choose from in the markets, and so many different flavours to use. If you have courgettes in the garden, and they have grown quicker than expected and turned into marrows, you can use them as well: just dice them very small, otherwise the chutney will become too wet.

main courses

fish

Monkfish with Artichoke Stuffing and White Wine Sauce 42
Seafood Marinière 43
Colcannon Haddock Fishcakes 44

Seafood Jambalaya 46
Haddock Fillets with Coriander and Lemon Pesto 47
Salcombe Salmon with Tiger Prawns 48

Monkfish with Artichoke Stuffing and White Wine Sauce

This is a lovely recipe which can be prepared in the dish, ready for the oven, with just the sauce to make. It is perfect for a special dinner party. Ask your fishmonger to fillet three monkfish tails, removing the bones, giving you six fillets.

Serves 6 Preparation time 10 minutes; Cooking time 20 minutes; Not suitable for freezing

butter
6 monkfish tail fillets (see above)
salt and pepper
6 thin long slices dry cured ham, eg Black
    Forest, Serrano or Parma
150 ml (5 fl oz) white wine
150 ml (5 fl oz) double cream
2 tablespoons snipped fresh chives

Topping
100 g (4 oz) artichoke hearts in oil from a
    jar, roughly chopped
2 tablespoons chopped fresh parsley
25 g (1 oz) fresh breadcrumbs

Preheat the oven to 180°C/350°F/Gas 4. Butter a roasting tin that will hold the fillets snugly in a single layer.

Arrange the monkfish in the buttered dish and season with salt and pepper.

Mix together all the ingredients for the topping and season with pepper (no salt, as the ham is salty). Divide the mixture into six and spoon on top of each monkfish fillet at the thick end. Wrap a piece of ham around the fish over the artichoke topping (so it is like a bandage, with the join underneath). Pour the wine around the edge of the dish (be careful not to pour it over the topping). Transfer to the preheated oven and bake for about 12–15 minutes until the fish is just done.

Carefully remove the fillets on to a plate while making the sauce. Bring the roasting tin to the boil over a high heat and boil so that the wine reduces by about half. Add the cream and boil for a couple of minutes to thicken slightly. Check for seasoning, sieve into a jug, and add the chives.

Serve one fillet per person with a little sauce.

To cook in the Aga Slide the dish on to the second set of runners in the roasting oven for about 12–15 minutes until the fish is just cooked.

Tip Be sure to buy artichokes in oil – they are much nicer than the ones in brine. Ask your fishmonger to remove the membrane from the monkfish. It is a grey slimy under-skin, which can be pulled off with a little persuasion. It must be removed as it restricts the fillets when cooking, making them shrivel. It doesn't taste very nice, either!

Seafood Marinière

This is very quick and easy to make, a little like the classic *moules marinière* that you can enjoy anywhere along the Channel coast of France. I think that it is lovely to serve certain dishes in a bowl and this recipe is perfect for that. It was very popular at work when I tested the recipe – it is rustic and has quite a thin creamy sauce, perfect for dipping the bread (see secret) into.

Serves 6 Preparation time 5–10 minutes: Cooking time about 5 minutes: Not suitable for freezing

6 shallots, finely chopped

2 cloves garlic, crushed

50 g (2 oz) white cup mushrooms, thinly sliced

150 ml (5 fl oz) white wine

300 ml (10 fl oz) pouring double cream

225 g (8 oz) monkfish, skinned and cut into 2.5 cm (1 in) dice

225 g (8 oz) raw tiger prawns, shelled

175 g (6 oz) cooked mussels, out of the shell

50 g (2 oz) baby spinach, very finely shredded

2 tablespoons chopped fresh dill

salt and pepper

Put the shallots, garlic, mushrooms, wine and cream into a wide-based saucepan and bring to the boil. Continue to boil over a high heat so the liquid reduces by half and thickens slightly.

Add the fish and seafood to the pan, cover and simmer over a low heat for about 2–3 minutes, until the prawns are pink and the fish is just cooked through.

Stir in the shredded spinach, dill and some salt and pepper, and boil for a further minute. Serve immediately with warm garlic herb bread (see secret).

To cook in the Aga Cook on the simmering plate as above.

Tip If you prefer, use raw mussels in their shells. Clean them well first. If they are open before they go into the sauce, and don't close when tapped, they are dead and should be thrown away.

a secret from our kitchen

The combination of the mussels with this bread is my idea of comfortable eating. To make garlic herb bread, slice a large white baguette on the diagonal into six thick slices. Mix 175 g (6 oz) soft butter with 3 crushed fat cloves of garlic and 2 tablespoons chopped fresh parsley, then season with salt and pepper. Thinly spread the butter on each side of the bread slices, and grill for about 5 minutes on each side until golden brown.

Colcannon Haddock Fishcakes

Finely shredded cabbage, mixed with potato as for colcannon, makes these fishcakes really delicious. You can use salmon instead of the haddock if you like.

Serves 6 Preparation time 20 minutes: Cooking time 20 minutes: Not suitable for freezing

450 g (1 lb) large potatoes, peeled and cut into chunks
salt and pepper
100 g (4 oz) Savoy cabbage, very finely shredded
melted butter
225 g (8 oz) smoked haddock fillets (undyed), skinned

225 g (8 oz) fresh haddock fillets, skinned
a squeeze of lemon juice
2 tablespoons low-calorie mayonnaise
1–2 tablespoons grainy mustard
2 tablespoons chopped fresh dill
about 50 g (2 oz) fresh breadcrumbs
paprika

Preheat the oven to 220°C/425°F/Gas 7.

Boil the potatoes in salted water for about 15 minutes or until they are nearly tender. Add the cabbage to the potatoes and continue to boil for a further 3 minutes until the potatoes are completely tender. Drain very well and set aside.

Butter a large piece of foil, place on a baking sheet and arrange the fish on top. Season with pepper and lemon juice. Wrap the foil tightly around the fish (so none of the juice escapes). Bake in the oven for 7–10 minutes until just cooked.

Remove the fillets from the foil and reserve the juices. Break the fish into large chunks into a mixing bowl (removing any bones). Set aside to cool.

Mash the potatoes and cabbage (the cabbage won't mash but it will mix in with the mashed potatoes). Stir in the fish juices, mayonnaise, mustard, dill, a little salt and pepper and the flaked fish. Set aside until cool enough to handle.

Divide and shape the mixture into 12 round cakes about 2.5 cm (1 in) deep: it is sticky, so do this with your hands. Pat the cakes all over in breadcrumbs. Lightly grease a baking sheet with butter. Arrange the cakes on top. Brush the tops of the cakes with a little melted butter and sprinkle with a touch of paprika.

Bake in the preheated oven for about 7–8 minutes, turn over and bake for a further 8 minutes or until golden brown all over. Serve hot with a herb salad.

To cook in the Aga
Cook the fish in foil in a roasting tin on the grid shelf on the floor of the roasting oven for about 7–10 minutes. Continue as above. Slide the baking sheet on to the floor of the roasting oven for about 5 minutes, turn the cakes over and bake for a further 5 minutes until golden brown all over.

Tip Instead of baking them in the oven you can fry them in a hot pan in a little butter – just until golden brown and hot right through.

Seafood Jambalaya

This warm, spicy Cajun dish is wonderful for all ages. Add more Tabasco if you like it extra hot! I am sorry there are lots of ingredients, but most of the dry ones you will have in your storecupboard already. The recipe really is worth it – all the flavours combined are delicious, and it is very quick and easy to do.

Serves 4 Preparation time 10 minutes: Cooking time 20 minutes: Not suitable for freezing

a secret from our kitchen

Parsley is my favourite herb and perfect for garnishing any dish. I have found the best way to keep chopped parsley fresh: cover with clingfilm in a bowl, pierce a few holes in the top and leave in the fridge – it will keep for a few days. Be sure to make holes in the clingfilm, though, otherwise the parsley will sweat and turn to compost!

2 tablespoons sunflower oil

1 large onion, coarsely chopped

1 fat clove garlic, crushed

1 x 2.5 cm (1 in) piece fresh root ginger, peeled and finely grated

2 sticks celery, finely chopped

1 teaspoon ground turmeric

1 teaspoon ground cumin

1 x 400 g can chopped tomatoes

1 litre (1³/4 pints) Vegetable Stock (see page 184)

1 teaspoon Tabasco sauce

300 g (10 oz) basmati rice

450 g (1 lb) raw mixed seafood (eg tiger prawns, squid rings, large mussels or clams)

2 tablespoons mango chutney

juice of ¹/2 lime

salt and pepper

2 tablespoons chopped fresh flat-leaf parsley

Heat the oil in a large non-stick frying pan, add the onion, garlic, ginger and celery, and fry over a high heat for a few minutes. Add the turmeric and cumin and stir for another minute or two. Blend in the tomatoes, stock and Tabasco and continue to cook for a few more minutes.

Stir in the rice, bring to the boil, cover and simmer for about 10–15 minutes until the stock has nearly been absorbed and the rice is just cooked.

Stir in the seafood, mango chutney and lime juice, and season with salt and pepper. Cook for a further 2–3 minutes until piping hot, sprinkle with parsley and serve.

To cook in the Aga After the rice has been stirred in, bring to the boil on the boiling plate and cook covered in the simmering oven for about 20 minutes until most of the liquid has been absorbed.

Tip If you haven't any turmeric or cumin in the cupboard you could use 2 teaspoons of garam masala or curry powder instead.

Haddock Fillets with Coriander and Lemon Pesto

A perfect quick recipe to make after a hard day's work. If liked, make double the amount of pesto and keep it in the fridge to use on pasta or to mix with a little crème fraîche to serve on the side.

Serves 4 Preparation time 4 minutes: Cooking time 10–15 minutes: Not suitable for freezing

4 x 150 g (5 oz) fresh haddock fillets, skinned
salt and pepper
1 lemon, quartered

Coriander pesto
a small bunch of fresh coriander
25 g (1 oz) pine nuts
25 g (1 oz) Parmesan cheese, freshly grated
juice of 1/2 lemon
4 tablespoons olive oil

a secret from our kitchen

The classic pesto is made with basil, but I think it's lovely to make different pestos, with alternate herbs – coriander as here, or flat-leaf parsley or rocket, for instance. Some herbs are stronger than others, so make to taste. Season well with salt and pepper as this brings out the flavour of the herbs.

Preheat the oven to 180°C/350°F/Gas 4.

Remove the stalks from the coriander and discard. Place the coriander leaves and all the remaining pesto ingredients in a processor and whizz for a few seconds until it becomes a coarse paste. Season well with salt and pepper.

Season the haddock fillets with salt and pepper. Divide the pesto into four and spread on to the top of each fillet. Take two small sheets of foil and place two fillets side by side in each piece. Turn up the edges so the top is still open but no juice can escape from the sides.

Transfer the foil to a baking sheet and bake in the preheated oven for about 10–12 minutes or until the fish is just cooked through. Serve hot with a squeeze of lemon on each.

To cook in the Aga Slide the baking sheet on to the lowest set of runners in the roasting oven for about 10 minutes until the fish is just cooked.

Tip Do be sure to buy fresh haddock and not smoked – smoked fish would not work well with pesto. If you buy tail fillets they may take a little less time to bake as they are slightly thinner – you can use any shape you like. You could choose sea bass or cod fillets instead of haddock if you prefer – they will take a little longer to cook.

Salcombe Salmon with Tiger Prawns

This very quick and attractive salmon recipe can be prepared ahead, and popped in the oven to serve. I first tested this in Salcombe in Devon, which is like my second home – I love visiting with family and friends and, in my opinion, it's the most beautiful place in the world. The coastline is second to none with hills, white sand beaches and the clear teal green water. It's still a fishing village with a wonderful history. I have even had the joy of seeing basking sharks and dolphins along the bay at Southsands and seals on the rocks across from Snapes Point.

Serves 4 Preparation time 10 minutes: Cooking time 15 minutes: Not suitable for freezing

4 x 150 g (5 oz) middle-cut fresh salmon fillets, skinned	Topping
	150 g (5 oz) Boursin cheese
salt and pepper	1 egg yolk
1 small packet plain potato crisps	1 tablespoon lemon juice
a little paprika	2 tablespoons chopped fresh parsley
fresh parsley, to garnish	12 cooked tiger prawns, shelled

Preheat the oven to 200°C/400°F/Gas 6.

For the topping, mix the Boursin, egg yolk, lemon juice and parsley together until smooth. Season to taste. Stir in the prawns so they are completely coated.

Arrange the salmon fillets on a baking sheet that you have lightly greased or lined with non-stick paper. Season with salt and pepper. Spoon the topping over the fillets evenly, making sure there are three prawns on each fillet. Sprinkle over some finely crushed crisps and dust with a little paprika.

Slide the baking sheet into the preheated oven and cook for about 12–15 minutes or until the salmon is completely cooked through. Serve immediately, garnished with parsley and a wedge of lemon.

To cook in the Aga Slide the baking sheet on to the second set of runners in the roasting oven for about 15 minutes or until just done.

Tip I prefer middle cut of salmon as it is taken from the centre of the fillet and therefore comes as a strip about 6 cm (2½ in) wide, which looks very attractive. It is important not to overcook fish, and unfortunately it so often is. If the fish is swimming in liquid it usually means it is overcooked. Cook until just done in the middle, still with a little moisture and not dry.

main courses

poultry and game

Pan-fried Chicken on Roasted Aubergine Boats

I had such fun devising this recipe. It is a meal in one, and for vegetarians, simply leave out the chicken – it's just as delicious. I have some friends who worked on an aubergine (eggplant) farm in the outback of Australia. Every day when working they popped a few in their pockets and lived off them for breakfast, lunch and supper. They had to leave after a month, as they couldn't look at another aubergine!

Serves 4 Preparation time 15 minutes: Cooking time about 45 minutes: Not suitable for freezing

2 tablespoons sunflower oil

4 large chicken breasts, boneless and
   skinless

2 small aubergines

2 medium courgettes, skin on, finely diced

2 tomatoes, finely chopped

1 red pepper, deseeded and finely
   chopped

2 cloves garlic, crushed

2 tablespoons Worcestershire sauce

1 tablespoon mango chutney

2 tablespoons tomato purée

2 tablespoons water

100 g (4 oz) mozzarella cheese, grated

salt and pepper

Preheat the oven to 200°C/400°F/Gas 6. You will need a shallow ovenproof dish that will hold the aubergine halves snugly in a single layer.

Heat 1 tablespoon of the oil in a large frying pan, and brown the chicken breasts on both sides over a high heat. Set aside.

Slice the aubergines in half lengthways. Using a teaspoon, scoop out and keep the flesh in the middle, leaving about 1 cm ($1/2$ in) thickness all around the edge and base of the aubergine. Arrange these aubergine boats snugly in a single layer in the ovenproof dish.

Add the remaining oil to the frying pan, and add the scooped-out aubergine flesh and the prepared vegetables. Stir-fry over a high heat for about 3 minutes. Add the remaining ingredients, except for the mozzarella, to the pan and stir over a high heat for a few minutes to evaporate any liquid. Season with salt and pepper.

Using a spoon, divide the mixture into four and use half to half-fill the aubergine boats. Top with mozzarella and spoon over the remaining mixture. Transfer to the preheated oven and bake for about 20 minutes.

Place a browned chicken breast on top of each aubergine, and return to the oven for a further 25 minutes until the chicken is completely cooked.

Slice each chicken breast into three, arrange these slices on top of each aubergine boat, and serve.

To cook in the Aga Brown the chicken in a frying pan on the boiling plate. Slide the ovenproof dish with the aubergine boats on to the grid shelf on the floor of the roasting oven, and roast for about 20 minutes. Place the chicken breasts on top of each boat, and return to the grid shelf on the floor of the roasting oven for a further 20–25 minutes or until the chicken is cooked through.

Tip Once the flesh has been scooped out of the aubergine it will go a little brown, but don't worry, this is fine. For slow cooking we always used to salt aubergine first to draw out any bitter juices. There's no need to do this nowadays as aubergines are picked much younger and therefore they are less bitter. Also, as you are adding the aubergine to the vegetables here, and stir-frying over a high heat, this will evaporate any juices that might be a little bitter.

Moroccan Chicken
with Couscous

This recipe only needs a vegetable with it, as the couscous replaces rice or potatoes. You could use chicken breasts instead of thighs if preferred. The couscous absorbs most of the liquid, but you do not need extra sauce with it.

Serves 4–6 Preparation time 15 minutes: Cooking time 35–40 minutes: To freeze see Tip below

1 tablespoon olive oil
8 chicken thighs, bone in, skinned
8 spring onions, sliced, keeping white and green parts separate
2 cloves garlic, crushed
1 large red pepper, deseeded and thinly sliced
1–2 tablespoons ground cumin

300 ml (10 fl oz) Chicken Stock (see page 184)
300 ml (10 fl oz) white wine
2 teaspoons runny honey
juice of $1/2$ lemon
salt and pepper
175 g (6 oz) couscous

a secret from our kitchen

If serving couscous as a side dish or for a salad, weigh 225 g (8 oz) couscous into a bowl, and cover with 300ml (10 fl oz) boiling stock and a tea-towel. Set aside until the couscous swells and the liquid has been absorbed, then puff up with a fork, and add all your favourite herbs and flavourings. I like to add masses of fresh mint and parsley, snipped apricots, cherry tomatoes, halved black olives and cubes of feta cheese with seasoning and a little salad dressing.

Heat the oil in a large non-stick frying pan over a high heat and brown the thighs all over until golden brown (you may need to do this in two batches). Set aside.

Add the white parts of the spring onion, the garlic and red pepper to the same pan, and fry over a high heat for about a minute. Sprinkle in the cumin, then blend in the stock, wine, honey and lemon juice. Season with salt and pepper, and stir over a high heat for a minute until it boils.

Return the chicken to the pan, bring back to the boil, cover with a lid and simmer over a low heat for about 30 minutes until the chicken is nearly tender.

About 5 minutes before the end of cooking, add the couscous to the frying pan and continue to cook, uncovered, for a further 5–7 minutes, stirring occasionally, until the couscous puffs up and is cooked and most of the liquid has been absorbed.

Stir in the green parts of the spring onions. Serve hot.

To cook in the Aga Brown the chicken in a non-stick frying pan on the boiling plate. Make the sauce as above on the boiling plate. Cover and transfer to the simmering oven for about 30 minutes until the chicken is nearly tender. Stir in the couscous and continue to cook, uncovered, in the simmering oven for a further 7 minutes until the couscous puffs up and is cooked.

Tip The couscous in this dish does not reheat well. To prepare it ahead (or freeze it), make the casserole and set aside (or freeze). To serve (defrost thoroughly if necessary), bring back to the boil, stir in the couscous and continue as above.

Chicken Milano
with Pesto Sauce

A wonderful Italian chicken breast recipe, which is perfect for a dinner party. You can stuff the chicken up to 12 hours ahead if time allows. The honey glaze helps the chicken to brown. You could use home-made pesto if you like (see page 47), but do be sure to make it with the traditional basil, not coriander.

Serves 6 Preparation time 20 minutes: Cooking time 35 minutes: Freezes well raw and stuffed. Sauce does not freeze

15 g (¹/₂ oz) butter
6 chicken breasts, boneless, skin on
salt and pepper
2 tablespoons runny honey
1 x 200 ml carton full-fat crème fraîche
2 tablespoons pesto from a jar

Stuffing
50 g (2 oz) butter
1 medium onion, finely chopped
3 slices Parma ham, snipped into small
  pieces
40 g (1¹/₂ oz) fresh white breadcrumbs
50 g (2 oz) Parmesan cheese, freshly
  grated
4 tablespoons chopped fresh parsley
1 egg, beaten

a secret from our kitchen

We find more and more that onions now have a tough outer layer under the outside skin, because they are often grown from sets and not seeds, and are therefore forced during growing. So remove this outer layer as well as the skin to be sure of perfectly tender onions after cooking. Or grow your own!

Preheat the oven to 200°C/400°F/Gas 6. Butter a small roasting tin.

To make the stuffing, melt the butter in a non-stick frying pan, add the onion and fry for a few minutes. Cover, lower the heat and cook for about 10–15 minutes until the onion is soft. Remove the lid, add the ham and fry over a high heat for a few minutes to crisp. Tip into a mixing bowl to cool. Add the breadcrumbs, Parmesan, parsley and egg to the mixing bowl, mix together and season with some salt and pepper.

Loosen the skin from the chicken breasts, leaving one side attached to make a small pocket. Season the chicken with salt and pepper. Divide the stuffing into six and stuff into the pocket in each piece of chicken. Pull the skin back over to cover the stuffing.

Arrange the chicken pieces snugly in the buttered roasting tin. Brush the skin on each breast with a little runny honey. Slide the tin into the preheated oven and bake for 20–25 minutes until the chicken is cooked and golden brown, and the juices run clear. Transfer to a plate and set aside to rest while you make the sauce.

Add the crème fraîche to the juices left in the tin. Scrape the bottom of the tin so all the juices and flavours are combined with the crème fraîche, and whisk

continued next page

over a high heat on the hob. Stir in the pesto and serve the sauce with the chicken breasts.

To cook in the Aga Cook the onion, covered, in the simmering oven for about 20 minutes until tender. Slide the chicken tin on to the highest set of runners in the roasting oven for about 15–20 minutes until the chicken is cooked and golden brown. Slide the sauce on to the floor of the roasting oven for about 3–5 minutes until bubbling.

Tip This recipe is delicious using boned quail or boned wood pigeon too. Rather than making just a few breadcrumbs, whizz a whole loaf in the processor and keep in the freezer. Use the crumbs straight from the freezer – they defrost very quickly. Never over-heat pesto sauce as it may become too oily.

Chicken Prosciutto au Vin

This is a variation on the classic French recipe for *coq au vin*, but using Italian dry-cured ham and red onions. You can use chicken breasts instead of thighs, if preferred.

Serves 4–6 Preparation time 10 minutes: Cooking time 20 minutes: Freezes well

1 tablespoon sunflower oil

8 chicken thighs, bone in, skinned

75 g (3 oz) dry-cured ham, such as Parma, Serrano or Black Forest, snipped into small pieces

2 cloves garlic, crushed

225 g (8 oz) button mushrooms, quartered

1 large red onion, coarsely chopped

1 tablespoon plain flour

300 ml (10 fl oz) Chicken Stock (see page 184)

300ml (10 fl oz) red wine

1 tablespoon Worcestershire sauce

1 tablespoon tomato purée

1 bay leaf

salt and pepper

2 tablespoons chopped fresh tarragon

Heat the oil in a large non-stick frying pan, and fry the chicken thighs on both sides until golden brown all over. Using a slotted spoon, transfer to a plate and set aside.

Add the ham to the same frying pan and fry over a high heat until crisp. Add the garlic, mushrooms and onion, and continue to fry for a few more minutes. Sprinkle in the flour and blend in the stock, wine, Worcestershire sauce and tomato purée. Add the bay leaf and some salt and pepper, and return the chicken to the pan. Bring to the boil, cover with a lid, then simmer over a low heat for about 45 minutes until the chicken is tender.

Add the tarragon and serve with rice or Creamy Celeriac Purée (see page 100).

To cook in the Aga Fry the chicken and make the sauce on the boiling plate. Cover and transfer to the simmering oven for about 45 minutes until the chicken is tender.

Tip The sauce may look fairly thick before the chicken is returned to the pan, but don't worry. During the 45 minutes' cooking, juices will come from the chicken, onions and mushrooms, and these will thin the sauce. The tarragon makes this recipe, so don't forget it!

a secret from our kitchen

We often cook a chicken dish for lunch at our demonstrations. When cooking for large numbers, make sure you fry the chicken breasts or thighs ahead in a frying pan until they are golden brown. Then cook them in the oven in the sauce in a large shallow dish. Too often chicken breasts are overcooked because they take time to brown in the oven, but if you brown them ahead, then you don't need to worry.

Roast Chicken with Lemon Herb Stuffing and Whisky Gravy

There is nothing nicer than a roast free-range chicken for Sunday lunch. I have made a fresh stuffing for it: it's not stodgy at all, just full of lovely flavours.

Serves 6 Preparation time 30 minutes: Cooking time about 2 hours: Not suitable for freezing

1 x 2 kg (4^1/$_2$ lb) free-range chicken
a little butter
Stuffing
1 tablespoon sunflower oil
2 onions, finely chopped
5 rashers unsmoked bacon, snipped into
   little pieces
40 g (1^1/$_2$ oz) fine fresh breadcrumbs
finely grated rind of 1 large lemon (reserve
   the lemon)
25 g (1 oz) pine nuts

4 sprigs of thyme, leaves only
   (reserve the stalks)
1 egg, beaten
salt and pepper
Gravy
25 g (1 oz) plain flour
2 tablespoons whisky
300 ml (10 fl oz) Chicken Stock
   (see page 184)
1 teaspoon Worcestershire sauce
1 tablespoon redcurrant jelly

Preheat the oven to 180°C/350°F/Gas 4.

To make the stuffing, heat the oil in a large non-stick frying pan, add the onion and bacon and fry over a high heat for a couple of minutes. Lower the heat, cover the pan, and soften the onion for about 20 minutes until tender. Turn up the heat and fry for a few minutes until crisp. Tip into a bowl. Add the remaining stuffing ingredients to the bowl, season with salt and pepper and set aside to cool. Cut six slices from the zested lemon, and cut the rest into wedges.

Working from the neck end of the bird, loosen the skin all over the breasts. Arrange the lemon slices under the skin. Take the stuffing in your hand and stuff at the same end of the bird, but just under the skin flap (not up over the breasts), shaping it with your hands, then fold the skin back under the bird. Sit the chicken in a roasting tin and arrange a few knobs of butter on the breast. Stuff the lemon wedges and thyme stems into the cavity of the bird.

Bake the chicken in the preheated oven for about 2 hours, or until the chicken juices run clear when a knife is inserted into the thigh. Set aside to rest while making the gravy.

To make the gravy, heat the roasting tin with all the juices on the hob and whisk in the flour (depending on the amount of fat in the tin, you may need a little more to make a loose roux). Add the remaining ingredients and boil to thicken, whisking all the time. Taste, and if a little sharp from the lemon, add a little more redcurrant jelly.

Serve the chicken with the gravy and stuffing, and some crisp roast potatoes.

To cook in the Aga To make the stuffing, soften the onion, covered, in the simmering oven for about 20 minutes. Add the bacon and fry for a few minutes on the boiling plate. Roast the chicken in a roasting tin on the lowest set of runners in the roasting oven for about 2 hours, or until the juices run clear. Add the ingredients for the gravy to the tin and transfer to the floor of the roasting oven for about 5 minutes until evenly boiling.

Tip If you do not wish to stuff the bird, shape the stuffing into six even-sized balls and arrange around the chicken 30 minutes before the end of cooking. Cook until crisp. If you are making a sausagemeat stuffing for a chicken or turkey, only stuff it under the skin at the neck end (as above). Don't ever put a meat stuffing in the cavity of the bird as it never gets hot enough to cook the stuffing thoroughly, and therefore can be a little dangerous to eat. I only ever put flavourings in the cavity of the bird.

Oven-roast Poussin with Orange, Garlic and Rosemary

Poussins are such delicious and easy birds to roast, and make a nice change from chicken (but you can also do this recipe with chicken if preferred). It's a perfect roast to do when you come in starving after a long walk in the autumn countryside. It doesn't take long to cook, and the smells from the kitchen are wonderful.

Serves 4–6 Preparation time 10 minutes plus marinating time: Cooking time 20 minutes: Not suitable for freezing

4 oven-ready poussins
300 ml (10 fl oz) orange juice from a
    carton
salt and pepper

Marinade

4 cloves garlic, crushed
3 tablespoons runny honey
3 tablespoons soy sauce
2 tablespoons olive oil
2 large sprigs fresh rosemary

First prepare the poussins. Place each bird upside down on a board. Using good scissors or poultry shears, carefully cut either side of the backbone and discard. Remove the wing tips if necessary and any loose skin.

Mix all the ingredients for the marinade in a bowl, add the poussins, and rub the marinade into the birds. Cover with clingfilm and leave to marinate for as long as time allows – a minimum of 2 hours preferably, or ideally overnight.

Preheat the oven to 200°C/400°F/Gas 6.

Remove the birds from the marinade (discard the rosemary sprigs, but keep the marinade for the sauce). Place the birds breast-side up in a roasting tin, so they fit snugly. Roast in the preheated oven for about 15–20 minutes until the poussins are cooked and the juices run clear when a knife is inserted into the thigh. Transfer the birds to a plate and set aside, covered in foil, to rest while making the sauce.

---

a secret from our kitchen

If your honey is cloudy and has set firm in the jar, take a spoonful out and heat it in the microwave. This will make it runny again. If you have an Aga, it's even easier. Sit the jar on the back of the Aga for a while, or in the simmering oven for 10 minutes.

Pour the reserved marinade into the hot roasting tin, add the orange juice and bring to the boil on the hob. Continue to boil for a good few minutes so the sauce reduces and thickens slightly, and is shiny. Season with salt and pepper, then sieve and keep warm.

To serve, cut the poussins in half through the breast bone, using good scissors or poultry shears, and give one or two halves per person (depending on appetite). Pour the sauce over the poussins.

To cook in the Aga Slide the roasting tin on to the top set of runners in the roasting oven for about 15–20 minutes until the poussins are cooked through and the juices run clear. To make the sauce, pour the marinade ingredients into the roasting tin and boil on the floor of the roasting oven for about 5 minutes until it has reduced slightly and is shiny.

Tip This is a thin sauce – there is no thickening agent – but it is full of flavour. Removing the backbone makes carving easier. To serve, all you need to do is cut through the breastbone with good scissors.

Thai Coconut Chicken

This recipe is quick to make, and has lots of flavour. The garnish makes it very pretty, so it's perfect for a dinner party. Thai sauces are traditionally thin; I have added just a little flour to make the sauce very slightly thicker than normal.

Serves 4 Preparation time 10 minutes: Cooking time 20 minutes: Not suitable for freezing

2 tablespoons sunflower oil
4 chicken breasts, boneless and skinless
salt and pepper
4 spring onions, thinly sliced on the
    diagonal
1/2 small red chilli, deseeded and very
    thinly sliced
1 x 2.5 cm (1 in) piece fresh root ginger,
    peeled and finely grated
1 tablespoon plain flour
1 x 400 ml can coconut milk

1 teaspoon red Thai curry paste
1 teaspoon caster sugar
1 stem fresh lemongrass, bashed with a
    rolling pin (but keep it whole)
juice of 1/2 lime

To garnish
2 spring onions, halved lengthways and
    cut into matchstick slices
1/2 small red chilli, deseeded and very
    thinly sliced
2 tablespoons chopped fresh coriander

a secret from
our kitchen

I adore fresh root ginger, it has such a fresh lemony smell. It is a perfect remedy for when you are feeling sick, or have a hangover. Rub a piece of peeled ginger on to the underside of your wrist for a few minutes. It really does help!

Heat 1 tablespoon of the oil in a large non-stick frying pan. Season the chicken breasts with salt and pepper, then brown them on each side over a high heat. Set aside while making the sauce.

Add the remaining oil to the pan, add the spring onion, chilli and ginger, and fry for couple of minutes. Sprinkle in the flour, and blend in the coconut milk, stirring continuously over a high heat. Bring to the boil, and stir in the curry paste, sugar and the whole stem of lemongrass. Season with salt and pepper.

Return the chicken to the pan, cover and simmer over a low heat for about 15–20 minutes until the chicken is cooked right through. Add the lime juice and check the seasoning. Remove the lemongrass and discard.

Slice the chicken breasts into three on the diagonal, arrange on individual plates, and spoon the sauce over the top. Garnish each plate with a pile of spring onions and chilli on top of the chicken, and sprinkle with coriander.

To cook in the Aga Bring to the boil on the boiling plate, cover and transfer to the simmering oven for about 20–25 minutes until the chicken is completely tender.

Tip Bruising the lemongrass with a rolling pin allows the flavour to permeate the sauce. Chopped lemongrass would not soften in the short cooking time, and would be too coarse to eat.

My Ma's Duck with Cherry Sauce

My lovely Ma used to cook duck with cherry sauce when she had friends over for dinner, so this recipe is dedicated to her. As kids, my three brothers and I used to do the washing up and finish off any food that was left, so I have fond memories of this recipe – and particularly of all the lovely puds, including a very naughty pineapple cream dessert which was so rich to eat I wouldn't be allowed to print it in a book!

Serves 4 Preparation time 5 minutes: Cooking time 5 minutes: Not suitable for freezing

4 duck breasts, skinless
a little soft butter
Sauce
150 ml (5 fl oz) red wine
150 ml (5 fl oz) water
150 ml (5 fl oz) cranberry juice

5 tablespoons Morello cherry jam
1–2 teaspoons balsamic vinegar
leaves from 3 sprigs fresh thyme
1 teaspoon cornflour, slaked with a little
   cold water
salt and pepper

To make the sauce, measure the wine, water, cranberry juice and jam into a saucepan and boil for about 5 minutes to reduce a little. Add the vinegar and thyme, stir in the slaked cornflour, and boil for a few more minutes over a high heat. Whisk until the sauce is smooth, then season with salt and pepper. Keep warm.

Heat a grill pan or frying pan until very hot. Spread a little butter on each side of the duck breasts. Brown the duck breasts on each side for 2 minutes (rare), 3–4 minutes (medium), or 5–6 minutes (well done – lower the heat when the breasts are brown).

Serve with the hot cherry sauce, adding any duck juices that have collected in the pan to the sauce.

To cook in the Aga Heat the grill pan on the floor of the roasting oven for 5 minutes until piping hot. Char-grill the duck in the pan on the boiling plate as above. Make the sauce as above on the boiling plate.

Tip Duck should be pink so don't overcook it, and it's accompanied here by a very quick sauce. Always mix cornflour with cold water, not hot, otherwise it will become lumpy. The cornflour gradually thickens the sauce as it is heated. If you want to prepare ahead, make the sauce up to 12 hours ahead, and reheat with any duck juices to serve.

a secret from our kitchen

When fresh cherries are in season, add a few fresh pitted ones to the sauce to make it extra special. Outside my office door at Mary's is a wall-climbing cherry. Unfortunately, we have trouble getting them to a ripe stage – even with netting, the birds get there first.

Mustard Pheasant with Chestnut and Apricot Crust

I have used pheasant breasts for this recipe, as they are quick to cook. The only way, in my opinion, to cook the legs from a whole bird is to casserole them long and slow to tenderise them. This dish can be made up to 24 hours ahead. Just put the crust on at the last minute to prevent it from going soggy.

Serves 4 Preparation time 15 minutes: Cooking time 20 minutes: Freezes well

butter
4 pheasant breasts, skinned
salt and pepper
1 tablespoon sunflower oil

Sauce
1 tablespoon sunflower oil
1 large onion, finely sliced
2 tablespoons paprika
300 ml (10 fl oz) double cream
2 tablespoons Dijon mustard

Crust
100 g (4 oz) cooked chestnuts, roughly
    chopped (see Tip)
50 g (2 oz) ready-to-eat dried apricots,
    finely snipped
25 g (1 oz) fresh breadcrumbs

Butter a 1.5 litre (2³/₄ pint) ovenproof dish.

Season the breasts with salt and pepper. Heat the oil in a large non-stick frying pan over a high heat, and fry the pheasant breasts on each side until golden brown. Remove from the pan and arrange in the ovenproof dish while making the sauce.

Heat the oil in the same pan, add the onion, lower the heat, cover and simmer for about 15 minutes until tender. Sprinkle the paprika over the onion and fry for a minute. Pour in the cream, add the mustard, season with salt and pepper, and boil for a minute or so. Set aside to cool.

Preheat the oven to 200°C/400°F/Gas 6.

To make the crust, mix all the ingredients together in a bowl and season well. Pour the cooled mustard sauce over the pheasant and sprinkle the crust over the top.

Bake in the preheated oven for about 15–20 minutes or until piping hot in the middle and the breasts are cooked through. The top will be nice and crispy too.

To cook in the Aga Soften the onion, covered, in a pan for about 20 minutes in the simmering oven. Continue as above on the boiling plate. To cook the whole dish, slide on to the second set of runners in the roasting oven for about 15 minutes until piping hot in the middle, the breasts are cooked through and the top is crisp.

Tip We always use frozen chestnuts, which are fantastic – they come ready to chop. In my opinion, they are much better than the vacuum-packed ones, which sometimes have a little skin still left on. I have said to cool the sauce before pouring on top of the breasts. This is especially important if you are preparing the dish ahead, as ideally the breasts and sauce should be the same temperature. If you are baking the dish straightaway in a hot oven, you don't need to worry too much.

Royal Berkshire Game Pie

a secret from our kitchen

Mary has a wonderful collection of old kitchen utensils, including some pie funnels – little ceramic blackbirds whose beaks poke through the pastry and allow the steam to escape during cooking. They are also used to help prevent the pastry from collapsing. Pastry in the old days was much thicker, and therefore heavier, so it needed supporting. This recipe has a fairly thin pastry topping, so doesn't really need supporting, but it all depends on the diameter of your pie dish. If you are worried your pastry may collapse, place an inverted cup into the pie dish and pour the casserole around it, making a couple of steam holes in the pastry on either side of the cup.

There is nothing like a game pie on a cold winter's day. I have used beef and venison for this recipe, with smoked bacon and prunes to add wonderful flavours. (You can use all beef, if preferred, but the recipe title would then have to be changed!) Serve with roasted country root vegetables, such as parsnips, swede and turnips.

Serves 6 Preparation time 20 minutes: Cooking time about 2 hours: Freezes well with raw pastry

3 tablespoons sunflower oil

450 g (1 lb) venison, diced into 2.5 cm (1 in) chunks

450 g (1 lb) braising steak, diced into 2.5 cm (1 in) chunks

75 g (3 oz) smoked bacon, rinded and cut into lardons

25 g (1 oz) butter

1 large onion, coarsely chopped

40 g (1 1/2 oz) plain flour

300 ml (10 fl oz) red wine

300 ml (10 fl oz) Beef or Game Stock (see page 184)

100 g (4 oz) closed cup mushrooms, quartered

2 tablespoons Worcestershire sauce

4 tablespoons cranberry sauce

100 g (4 oz) dried pitted prunes, quartered

salt and pepper

Pastry

225 g (8 oz) plain flour

100 g (4 oz) butter

2 eggs

You will need a 1.5 litre (2 3/4 pint) pie dish, not too shallow, about 23 cm (9 in) in diameter.

Heat 2 tablespoons of the oil in a large non-stick frying pan, and seal the venison and beef over a high heat until brown all over (you may need to do this in batches). Using a slotted spoon, remove the meat and set aside. Add the bacon to the pan and brown over a high heat until crisp. Set aside with the venison and beef.

Heat the remaining oil and the butter together in the same pan, and fry the onion for a few minutes over a high heat. Return the meats to the pan, sprinkle in the flour, and gradually blend in the wine and stock. Stirring continuously, bring to the boil over a high heat. Add the mushrooms, Worcestershire sauce, cranberry sauce, prunes and some salt and pepper. Boil for a few minutes, then lower the heat, cover and simmer for about 1½ hours until the meats are tender. Check the seasoning and set aside to cool while making the pastry.

To make the pastry, measure the flour and butter into a processor and whizz for a few minutes until the mixture resembles breadcrumbs. Add one of the eggs, mixed with 2 tablespoons water, and whizz again until the ingredients come together and form a ball of dough. Wrap in clingfilm and rest in the fridge for 30 minutes, if time allows.

Preheat the oven to 180°C/350°F/Gas 4.

Spoon the casserole into the pie dish. Roll out the pastry to the size of the pie dish. Wet the edges of the pie dish and lay the pastry over the top of the dish, pressing along the rim to seal. Trim the edges and re-roll the trimmings and use for pastry leaves as a garnish. Brush the pastry with the remaining egg, which you have beaten. Arrange pastry leaves on top and brush them with beaten egg as well. Using a knife, make a small hole in the centre of the pastry.

Transfer to the preheated oven and bake for about 40 minutes until the pastry is golden and the pie is piping hot.

To cook in the Aga Make the casserole as above. Bring to the boil on the boiling plate, cover and transfer to the simmering oven for about 1½–2 hours until the meats are tender. Continue as above. Slide the pie dish on to the grid shelf on the floor of the roasting oven and cook for about 25 minutes. Check after 10 minutes and turn around. If the pastry is getting too brown, slide the cold sheet on to the second set of runners.

Tip It is important to make a small hole in the pastry before cooking in the oven. This allows the steam to escape and prevents the pastry from becoming soggy. You can use bought shortcrust pastry if preferred – roll out fairly thinly.

main
courses

meat

Bachelor's Beef

I invented this recipe for a local friend who was on his own and needed looking after. I simply opened my storecupboard and threw in anything I had, but luckily all the ingredients were those that men love, including chilli and kidney beans! Serve with vegetables and mash.

Serves 6 Preparation time 15 minutes: Cooking time about 2 hours: Freezes well without the horseradish sauce

2 tablespoons sunflower oil

900 g (2 lb) braising steak, cut into
   2.5 cm (1 in) cubes

2 cloves garlic, crushed

2 small leeks, thinly sliced

225 g (8 oz) button mushrooms, quartered

1 yellow pepper, deseeded and thinly
   sliced

2 tablespoons plain flour

1 teaspoon mild chilli powder

150 ml (5 fl oz) red wine

1 x 400 g can chopped tomatoes

1 tablespoon Worcestershire sauce

1 tablespoon redcurrant jelly

1 x 400 g can kidney beans, drained and
   rinsed

salt and pepper

2 tablespoons horseradish sauce

Heat 1 tablespoon of the oil in a deep saucepan and fry the meat until sealed and golden brown (you may need to do this in batches). Add the remaining oil, along with the garlic, leeks, mushrooms and pepper and fry over a high heat for a few minutes.

Sprinkle in the flour and chilli powder, then stir in the wine, chopped tomatoes, Worcestershire sauce, redcurrant jelly and kidney beans and bring to the boil. Season with salt and pepper and simmer over a low heat for about $1^1/_2$–2 hours until the meat is tender.

Serve with a dollop of horseradish sauce on top of each portion.

To cook in the Aga Fry the meat on the boiling plate, then add the remaining ingredients. Bring to the boil, cover and transfer to the simmering oven for about 2–$2^1/_2$ hours until the meat is tender.

Tip Use stewing or braising steak. There's no need to buy an expensive cut of beef as the slow cooking will tenderise the meat. Chilli powders come in different strengths – if you only have the hot variety just use a pinch. But if you like it extra hot, you could also use a hot variety of horseradish cream.

Steak à la Ramatuelle

Ramatuelle is a wonderful village in the hills of the South of France, which I've been visiting for an annual holiday for many years: it's like an addiction. It's a magical place to me, with the countryside, lavender fields and vineyards. Ramatuelle has a little market square, next to the church, and on Tuesdays there is a typical French market selling honey, olive oil, tablecloths, balsamic vinegar, pottery and much more (over the years I've bought just about everything on offer). Next to the market the men play boules, taking about three hours for one game – so traditionally French!

Serves 4 Preparation time 10 minutes: Cooking time 18 minutes: Not suitable for freezing

1 tablespoon sunflower oil
4 x 175 g (6 oz) fillet steaks, about 5 cm
   (2 in) thick
3 shallots, very finely chopped
1 level tablespoon paprika

300 ml (10 fl oz) red wine
150 ml (5 fl oz) Beef Stock (see page 184)
1 teaspoon caster sugar
salt and pepper

Heat the oil in a large non-stick frying pan over a high heat, and sear the steaks on one side for about a minute until golden brown. Remove and set aside.

Add the shallots to the pan, lower the heat, cover and cook for about 10 minutes until soft. Remove the lid, turn up the heat, and sprinkle in the paprika. Blend in the wine and stock, bring to the boil for a couple of minutes, stirring, then sprinkle in the sugar.

Return the steaks, browned side up, to the pan and cook over a low bubbling heat for about 8–10 minutes (rare), 10–12 minutes (medium) or 13–15 minutes (well done). Season to taste.

Remove the steaks from the pan, and serve either whole or carve into three on the diagonal. Serve with Herby Parsnip and Potato Cakes (see page 101) and with the sauce.

To cook in the Aga Soften the shallots, covered, in the simmering oven for about 10 minutes. Continue on the simmering plate.

Tip You can also use rib-eye steak for this recipe (because of the short cooking time, a good cut of meat is needed). Cooking times may vary depending on the thickness of the steak. Use a frying pan with as wide a base as possible – this will enable the sauce to reduce more quickly. If you use a smaller pan, remove the steaks, keep them warm, and reduce the sauce over a high heat until shiny and the right consistency.

a secret from our kitchen

When freezing home-made stock, it's a great idea to freeze it in clean cream pots of 150 ml (5 fl oz or 1/4 pint) and 300 ml (10 fl oz or 1/2 pint) capacities – then you will have the exact quantity you need for a recipe.

Cumberland Sausage Cassoulet

This recipe is a modern version of the French classic, very rustic looking but full of flavour. A traditional cassoulet is a dish made with haricot beans and meat – usually pork or mutton, goose or pork. My variation has been tested many times by my gorgeous little brother, Chris, and his lovely wife, Nik. It will become a firm favourite of yours, I'm sure.

Serves 6 Preparation time 15 minutes: Cooking time about 1½ hours: Freezes well

12 Cumberland or well-flavoured sausages
1 tablespoon sunflower oil
6 shallots, halved
225 g (8 oz) unsmoked bacon lardons
2 cloves garlic, crushed
1 tablespoon plain flour
450 ml (15 fl oz) white wine
150 ml (5 fl oz) water

1 x 400 g can borlotti or cannellini beans, drained and rinsed
1 x 400 g can chopped tomatoes
2 tablespoons tomato purée
1 tablespoon each of chopped fresh sage, rosemary and thyme
salt and pepper

a secret from our kitchen

If you prefer, use cocktail sausages. I have tried this, and it is just as delicious, but they must be well-flavoured, good-quality sausages.

Cut each sausage into three pieces. Heat the oil in a deep non-stick frying pan and fry the sausages over a high heat until brown and crisp (you may need to do this in batches, removing some of the fat left in the pan with each batch). Remove with a slotted spoon and set aside. Pour off the fat, leaving about a tablespoon in the frying pan.

Add the shallots, bacon and garlic to the fat in the pan, and fry for a few minutes until brown. Stir in all the remaining ingredients, and season with salt and pepper. Pour into a casserole dish if the frying pan is not deep enough. Return the sausages to the dish or pan, cover, and simmer over a low heat on the hob for about 1½ hours until the sausages are tender.

Serve with mustard mash and French beans.

To cook in the Aga Brown the sausages in a non-stick frying pan on the boiling plate. Continue as above, bring to the boil, cover and cook in the simmering oven for about 1½–2 hours until tender.

Tip The sausages do need to be browned very well as they don't look very attractive if they are pale. Do be sure to drain off the fat after frying or, if need be, at the end of cooking.

Salt Beef and Winter Vegetables with Mustard and Horseradish Sauce

This is an old-fashioned dish, which I have modernised by adding a full flavoured sauce. It is very trendy again in all the top restaurants! I have used silverside of beef, which is the cut of meat under topside. The slow poaching method ensures that it is very tender. The meat has been salted, which semi-cures it. You can soak the beef to remove a little excess salt before cooking if liked, but check with your butcher as he will know how salty the cure was.

Serves 6 Preparation time 25 minutes: Cooking time 3 hours: Not suitable for freezing

1.3 kg (3 lb) salted silverside of beef
8 baby shallots, left whole
6 medium turnips, peeled and quartered
450 g (1 lb) baby carrots
225 g (8 oz) potatoes, peeled and cut into
  5 cm (2 in) pieces
3 tablespoons chopped fresh parsley

Sauce
450 ml (15 fl oz) double cream
4 tablespoons creamy horseradish sauce
2 tablespoons grainy mustard
salt and pepper

Place the beef in a deep saucepan and just cover with cold water. Cover with the lid and bring to the boil. Lower the heat and leave to simmer for about 2½ hours.

Bring back to the boil, and add the prepared vegetables. Lower the heat again, and continue to simmer for a further 30 minutes or until the vegetables are tender.

Meanwhile make the sauce. Measure the cream into a saucepan and boil for about 5 minutes until it has reduced slightly and has started to thicken. Stir in the horseradish and mustard and season with salt and pepper.

Remove the beef from the saucepan and set aside to rest for a few moments. Drain the vegetables, pile them into a serving dish, and sprinkle over the parsley. Thinly carve the beef, and serve with the vegetables and hot sauce.

To cook in the Aga Place the beef in a deep saucepan and just cover with cold water. Bring to the boil on the boiling plate, cover and transfer to the simmering oven for about 2½ hours. Add the vegetables, bring back to the boil on the boiling plate, cover and return to the simmering oven for a further 35 minutes until the vegetables are just cooked.

Tip You can use Dijon mustard rather than grainy mustard if preferred, but I like the texture of grainy mustard. If you only have hot strong horseradish, add to taste. The poaching liquid is thrown away as it is too salty to use for a sauce. It is important for meat to rest before carving. This sets the juices, thereby keeping the joint moist and making the carving easier.

Mild Curry in a Hurry

Sorry about the title, but we had a good laugh choosing it! The recipe is very quick and easy to do, with the flavours a mixture between Thai and Indian curry. Serve with some boiled rice and prawn crackers.

Serves 4–6 Preparation time 10 minutes: Cooking time 10 minutes: Not suitable for freezing

3 tablespoons sunflower oil

450 g (1 lb) pork fillet, sliced into thin strips

1 onion, finely chopped

1 clove garlic, crushed

1 small red chilli, deseeded and finely chopped

1 tablespoon medium curry powder

1 x 400 g can chopped tomatoes

1 x 400 ml can coconut milk

finely grated zest and juice of 1 lime

salt and pepper

2 spring onions, finely sliced, to garnish

Heat 2 tablespoons of the oil in a non-stick frying pan and brown the pork over a high heat until golden brown all over (you may need to do this in batches). Remove from the pan using a slotted spoon and set aside while you make the sauce.

Add the remaining oil to the pan and fry the onion, garlic and chilli over a high heat for a few minutes. Sprinkle over the curry powder and cook for a few minutes, then add the tomatoes and coconut milk, and stir while the sauce comes to the boil. Lower the heat slightly so that the sauce is still bubbling gently, and allow to reduce slightly for about 5 minutes.

Return the pork to the pan and continue to cook over the same heat, without a lid, for a further 5 minutes or so or until the pork is tender (this will depend on the thickness of your strips).

Add the lime zest and juice to the pan, and season with salt and pepper. Serve immediately, garnished with the spring onions.

To cook in the Aga Fry the pork in a non-stick frying pan on the boiling plate, then set aside. Make the sauce as above, then transfer to the simmering oven, without a lid, for about 5 minutes. Return to the boiling plate, add the pork, and bring back to the boil. Return to the simmering oven, without a lid, for a further 5 minutes or so until the pork is tender.

Tip To begin with, the sauce is a little thin, which is why I suggest cooking without the lid. This allows the sauce to reduce a little and thicken.

Roast Loin of Pork with Pear, Sage and Roasted Vegetables

Sage and onion stuffing is a natural with pork, so I have used this idea in a slightly different way. I have added the flavours to the roasting tin, along with the pork and vegetables, which means you only have to cook some green vegetables separately. This would be perfect for a Sunday lunch.

Serves 6 Preparation time 20 minutes: Cooking time about 1 $^1/_2$ hours: Not suitable for freezing

You can peel potatoes and parsnips ahead and keep them covered in water in the fridge for up to a day before they are used. Peeled and cut potatoes and parsnips will discolour when left without water in a bowl as the oxygen in the air affects them. If you cover them with water, they will be fine. Blanching the vegetables ahead means you can have pre-prepared quite a proportion of this recipe in advance. You then just need to pop them in the oven to roast.

2 kg (4$^1/_2$ lb) boned loin of pork, with skin scored finely for crackling
sunflower oil
sea salt
2 Spanish onions
4 large (about 750 g/1$^3/_4$ lb) potatoes
4 large parsnips
2 large carrots
4 tablespoons coarsely chopped fresh sage
3 just ripe fresh pears, peeled and diced

Sauce
a good tablespoon plain flour
about 300 ml (10 fl oz) cider or apple juice
2 tablespoons apple sauce from a jar

Preheat the oven to 200°C/400°F/Gas 6.

Lay the pork, fat-side up, on a work surface. Brush a little oil over the skin and press on crystals of sea salt. Pour a couple of tablespoons of oil into the base of a large roasting tin. Slide the tin into the preheated oven for about 10 minutes until the oil is piping hot.

Cut the onions into thick wedges. Peel and cut the other vegetables into even-sized pieces (about 5 cm/2 in square). Blanch the vegetables (not the onions) in boiling, salted water for about 5 minutes, then drain and refresh in cold water until stone cold (this can be done well in advance).

When the fat is hot, put the pork into the centre of the roasting tin. Return to the oven for about 30 minutes. Arrange the onions and blanched vegetables around the pork, coat in the hot fat, then cook for a further hour until the vegetables are tender, the pork is cooked and the crackling is crisp.

Remove the pork and set aside, covered, to rest. Using a slotted spoon, transfer the vegetables to a serving dish. Mix in the diced pears and sage. Cover and keep warm in a low oven.

To make the sauce, sprinkle the flour into the remaining fat in the tray to form a soft roux. Place the roasting tin over a high heat and gradually add the cider or apple juice, whisking all the time. Add the apple sauce and some salt and pepper. Bring to the boil and taste (add a little more apple sauce if liked), then sieve.

Carve the pork and crackling into thin slices and serve with the sauce and the roasted vegetables.

To cook in the Aga Slide the pork in the roasting tin on to the second set of runners of the roasting oven for about 30 minutes, then arrange the onions and blanched vegetables around the pork and roast for a further hour until the pork is cooked, the crackling crisp and vegetables roasted. If the crackling is really crisp, but the vegetables aren't quite brown enough, slide the tin directly on to the floor of the roasting oven to brown the vegetables a bit more.

Tip You can use alternative root vegetables if preferred, but ensure that they are all cut to the same size so that the cooking time is the same.

Coriander Crushed Pork Chops with Piquant Red Pepper Sauce

I have used boneless loin pork chops for this recipe as I think they have better flavour and are larger than the standard pork chops. Ask your butcher to cut them from the thick end of the loin. The sauce is a fairly thick purée.

Serves 4 Preparation time 15 minutes: Cooking time about an hour (including the sauce): Not suitable for freezing

2 tablespoons coriander seeds
4 pork loin chops, fat trimmed
2 tablespoons olive oil
Sauce
8 large tomatoes
3 large red peppers

1 small red chilli
1 tablespoon olive oil
1 teaspoon balsamic vinegar
a small knob of butter
salt and pepper

To start the sauce, roughly chop the tomatoes (including the seeds). Cut the red peppers in half, remove the seeds and cores, then roughly chop the flesh. Deseed and finely chop the chilli.

Heat the oil in a non-stick frying pan, add the tomato, pepper and chilli, and fry over a high heat for a minute. Lower the heat, cover and simmer for about an hour, until soft and mushy. Sieve over a pan, discarding the pulp left in the sieve. Add the balsamic vinegar to the purée in the pan, bring to the boil and whisk in the butter. Keep warm.

Crush the coriander seeds in a pestle and mortar (or place in a plastic bag and bash with a rolling pin) until broken up but still coarse. Brush each pork chop with oil and press the coriander seeds on to the chops on both sides.

Heat a large non-stick frying pan until very hot. Arrange the chops in a single layer and lower the heat. Cook the chops for 5 minutes on each side or until cooked (the juices are not bloody) and they are golden brown on each side.

Serve the chops with the hot sauce on the side.

To cook in the Aga Cook the sauce, covered, in the simmering oven for about an hour, or until soft and mushy. Preheat a non-stick frying pan on the floor of the roasting oven for about 5 minutes to get it very hot. Carefully remove from the oven and place on the simmering plate. Cook the pork chops for 5 minutes on each side until golden brown and cooked through.

Paprika Spiced Lamb

This recipe has a mild spiciness to it. It's a wonderful curry to make in advance and serve, say, when you come home from the pub, as it only needs reheating and can be accompanied with quickly cooked rice or mash.

Serves 6 Preparation time 15 minutes: Cooking time 1½ hours: Freezes well

2 tablespoons sunflower oil

900 g (2 lb) lamb neck fillet, cut into
  2.5 cm (1 in) dice

2 large onions, thickly sliced

1 x 7.5 cm (3 in) piece fresh root ginger,
  peeled and grated

2 tablespoons garam masala

1 tablespoon paprika

150 ml (5 fl oz) white wine

1 x 400 g can chopped tomatoes

2 tablespoons tomato purée

2 tablespoons mango chutney

salt and pepper

a little Greek yoghurt (optional)

Heat 1 tablespoon of the oil in a large non-stick frying pan and fry the meat on all sides until golden brown (you may need to do this in batches). Set aside.

Heat the remaining oil in the same frying pan, add the onion and ginger, and fry for a couple of minutes. Return the meat to the pan, sprinkle in the garam masala and paprika to coat the meat, and fry for a minute. Blend in the wine, chopped tomatoes, tomato purée and mango chutney. Bring to the boil, season with salt and pepper, cover and cook over a low heat for about 1½–2 hours or until the meat is tender.

Serve with a dollop of yoghurt, if liked.

To cook in the Aga Make as above. Bring to the boil on the boiling plate, cover and cook in the simmering oven for about 1½–2 hours or until the meat is tender.

Tip Neck of lamb fillet is the perfect cut to braise or cook for a long time. Do not get it muddled with the loin fillet, which is a very delicate cut that only needs a short cooking time and is very expensive! Garam masala is a well-used spice, a mixture of cloves, cinnamon, coriander, cumin, turmeric, cardamom and dill seeds. All these together give an authentic curry flavour, which I personally prefer to curry powder, but you could use curry powder instead if liked.

Garlic Rack of Lamb with Mint and Sun-blushed Tomato Sauce

This is an unusual sauce to serve with rack of lamb as it is creamy, a bit like a paloise sauce. It's also delicious with saddle of lamb, a cut that is too often forgotten: although expensive, it's fantastic for a dinner party.

Serves 4–6 Preparation time 10 minutes: Cooking time 25 minutes: Not suitable for freezing

a secret from our kitchen

The anchovies really make the sauce, and give a very subtle flavour. When testing, I made two sauces: one with anchovies, and one without. We did a blind tasting with the girls at work, and even though most of them don't like anchovies, they all preferred the one with.

2 racks of lamb, 7 chops in each,
  chine bone cut through
4 cloves garlic, quartered
fresh mint sprigs, to garnish
Sauce
300 ml (10 fl oz) double cream
2 cloves garlic, halved

3 anchovy fillets
150 ml (5 fl oz) white wine
1 good teaspoon mint sauce from a jar
2 tablespoons chopped fresh mint
50 g (2 oz) sun-blushed tomatoes, snipped
salt and pepper

Preheat the oven to 200°C/400°F/Gas 6.

Remove any excess fat from the racks of lamb. At irregular intervals pierce eight holes through the fat of each rack using a sharp knife – make sure the hole goes into the meat. Stud a piece of garlic into each hole.

Transfer the racks to a roasting tin, skin-side up, and roast in the preheated oven for about 20–25 minutes or until just done (lamb should be served pink in the middle). Check after 15 minutes: if getting too brown, cover with a piece of foil.

Meanwhile, to make the sauce, measure the cream into a saucepan, add the garlic and anchovies, and bring to the boil. Cover and simmer over a low heat for about 15–20 minutes or until the garlic is soft and squidgy. Sieve (pressing the garlic through with the back of a spoon) into a clean saucepan, then add the wine and bring to the boil. Reduce over a high heat for about 2 minutes, stirring all the time so the sauce does not stick. Add the mint sauce, chopped fresh mint, tomatoes and some salt and pepper to taste.

Just before carving, rest the lamb for a few minutes covered in foil. Remove the chine bone, carve between the bones and arrange the little chops on a plate. Serve with the hot sauce, garnished with the fresh sprigs of mint.

To cook in the Aga Put the lamb in a small roasting tin and roast on the top set of runners in the roasting oven for about 20–25 minutes until just tender and

continued next page

pink in the middle. Remove the lamb from the tin, transfer to a plate and cover with foil to rest. Bring the first stage of the sauce to the boil on the boiling plate, cover and transfer to the simmering oven for about 20 minutes for all the flavours to infuse. Continue as above, and reduce on the boiling plate for about 2 minutes.

Tip Ask your butcher to French trim your racks (short bones) and to cut the chine bone through, as this makes carving easier. The latter needs to be done with a saw, so is quite difficult to do at home! Often when you buy pre-packed racks, the chine bone has been removed. This is fine for this recipe, but if you are making a crown roast, you need the chine bone for the crown to sit on.

Lamb Shanks with Country Vegetables and Red Wine Sauce

Lamb shanks are very popular in restaurants, whether in the city or in the country, and when cooked correctly there is nothing nicer – the meat should be just falling off the bone. Some shanks you buy from the butcher are very large, so just be aware of your guests' appetites when choosing them.

Serves 4 Preparation time 20 minutes: Cooking time about 3 hours: Freezes well

a secret from our kitchen

If you have any wine left over (not if you're in my family!), pour into ice-cube trays and freeze. You can then simply pop a cube from the tray to use for your next recipe.

2 tablespoons sunflower oil
4 lamb shanks
8 small shallots
6 sticks celery, cut into 5 cm (2 in) batons
225 g (8 oz) baby carrots, halved lengthways
2 fat cloves garlic, crushed
4 tablespoons plain flour

300 ml (10 fl oz) red wine
2 x 400 g cans chopped tomatoes
2 tablespoons redcurrant jelly
salt and pepper
225 g (8 oz) button mushrooms
3 good tablespoons chopped fresh rosemary

Heat 1 tablespoon of the oil in a large non-stick frying pan and sear the lamb shanks over a high heat until brown on all sides (you may need to do this in batches). Transfer the shanks to a deep casserole with a lid.

Heat the remaining oil in the same frying pan, add the whole shallots, the celery, carrots and garlic, and fry over a high heat for a few minutes. Sprinkle in the flour to coat the vegetables, then slowly stir in the wine, tomatoes and redcurrant jelly. Bring to the boil, stirring continuously, then boil for a few minutes until the liquid thickens slightly. Season with salt and pepper.

Pour the sauce over the shanks in the casserole, bring to the boil, cover and simmer over a low heat for about 1¹/₂ hours, stirring occasionally.

Stir in the mushrooms and continue to cook, covered, for a further 1¹/₂ hours until the shanks are tender and the meat is just falling off the bone.

Check the seasoning, stir in the rosemary and serve with mashed potato.

To cook in the Aga Brown the lamb and make the sauce on the boiling plate. Bring to the boil, cover, and transfer to the simmering oven for about 1¹/₂ hours. Add the mushrooms, bring to the boil again on the boiling plate, cover and return to the simmering oven for a further 1¹/₂ hours or until the meat is just falling off the bone.

Tip It is important to brown the lamb first as this seals the juices in the meat. Buy lamb shanks all the same size so they cook at the same rate. Don't forget to add the rosemary – it makes the recipe.

vegetables

and vegetarian

Vegetarian Lentil and Spinach en Croûte (V) 90

Portobella Mediterranean Mushrooms (V) 91

Four Cheese Spinach Quiche (V) 92

Honey-roasted Butternut Squash Risotto (V) 94

Chunky Veggie Tagine (V) 96

Braised Red Cabbage with Beetroot and Cranberries (V) 98

Roasted Sweet Potatoes with Orange, Chilli and Coriander (V) 99

Creamy Celeriac Purée (V) 100

Herby Parsnip and Potato Cakes (V) 101

Vegetarian Lentil and Spinach en Croûte

This combination of vegetables, lentils, pastry and cheese is perfect for a vegetarian supper. Just serve with a dressed salad. The completed en croûte can be made up to 24 hours ahead and kept in the fridge.

Serves 6 Preparation time 30 minutes: Cooking time 30 minutes: Not suitable for freezing

a secret from our kitchen

Season the mixture well with salt and pepper – lentils and most pulses need a lot of seasoning after they have been cooked. Don't season them before as the skins harden and become even drier.

150 g (5 oz) dried Puy lentils
1 tablespoon olive oil
100 g (4 oz) chestnut mushrooms, sliced
150 g (5 oz) baby spinach, roughly chopped
150 g (5 oz) mixed char-grilled peppers from a jar, cut into large pieces

2 tablespoons curry powder
2 tablespoons mango chutney
salt and pepper
1 x 375 g packet ready-rolled puff pastry
50 g (2 oz) mature Cheddar cheese, grated
1 egg, beaten

Preheat the oven to 200°C/400°F/Gas 6, and heat a baking sheet to get very hot.

Rinse the lentils under water and drain. Put the lentils in a saucepan, cover with cold water, bring to the boil, then simmer over a low heat, covered, for about 15–20 minutes or until just tender. Drain and refresh in cold water.

Heat the oil in large non-stick frying pan, add the mushrooms and fry over a high heat for a minute. Add the spinach and peppers and fry for a further minute. Sprinkle in the curry powder and stir in the mango chutney and lentils. Season with salt and pepper and set aside to get cold.

Flour a worktop and roll the pastry to 30 x 38 cm (12 x 15 in). Arrange half the cold lentil mixture in the centre of the pastry, sprinkle over the cheese, and spoon the remaining mixture on top of the cheese. Fold up the short edges of the pastry over the mixture. Brush the long edges with a little beaten egg and bring up so they meet in the centre. Seal the edges together in a crimp, so it looks like a strudel with a crimped top. Brush with beaten egg.

Carefully transfer to the hot baking sheet in the preheated oven, and bake for about 30 minutes until the pastry is golden brown and crisp underneath.

To cook in the Aga Slide the en croûte on the baking sheet (it doesn't need to be hot) directly on to the floor of the roasting oven for about 30–35 minutes until the pastry is golden brown and crisp underneath.

Tip Cook the filling mixture in a wide-based pan so any liquid evaporates off. The mixture should be fairly dry, otherwise the pastry will become soggy.

Portobella Mediterranean Mushrooms

(V)

Portobella mushrooms are a large variety of flat field mushroom. After warm weather in the early autumn, it is fun to go mushrooming in the woods, as you can find some wonderful field mushrooms. Buy a good book on mushrooms, though, to check that they are safe to eat. Most are, but there are a few that are to be avoided! The mushrooms look wonderful on a buffet table, and they can be served for a barbecue. Of course, they are perfect for a starter or light supper too.

Serves 6 Preparation time 10 minutes: Cooking time 25 minutes: Not suitable for freezing

6 large flat field mushrooms, eg portobella (all the same size)
3 tablespoons olive oil
salt and pepper
2 large red onions, cut into wedges
2 cloves garlic, crushed

300 g (10 oz) char-grilled mixed peppers in oil from a jar, drained and chopped into large pieces
25 g (1 oz) fresh breadcrumbs
25 g (1 oz) Gruyère cheese, grated
paprika

Preheat the oven to 200°C/400°F/Gas 6.

Carefully remove the stalks from the mushrooms. Heat 2 tablespoons of the oil in a large non-stick frying pan and fry the mushrooms over a high heat on each side for a few minutes until nearly tender and brown. Season with salt and pepper. Transfer the mushrooms (gill side up) to a shallow ovenproof dish so they are in a single layer.

Heat the remaining oil in the pan, and cook the onion wedges for about 5 minutes or until golden brown but still slightly crunchy. Add the garlic, and season with salt and pepper.

Divide the onion mixture between the six mushrooms, spooning it over the top of each one. Top with char-grilled peppers, breadcrumbs and cheese. Just before cooking sprinkle with a little paprika.

Bake in the preheated oven for 15–20 minutes until piping hot and crispy brown on top. Serve immediately with a fresh dressed green herb salad.

To cook in the Aga Bake the mushrooms on the second set of runners in the roasting oven for about 15–20 minutes until golden brown.

Tip To prepare ahead, cover the completed dish with clingfilm and keep in the fridge for up to 24 hours. Reheat from room temperature as above.

Four Cheese Spinach Quiche

A quiche is a classic French country recipe. You can use virtually anything in the filling, and it is a perfect way in which to feed quite large numbers. I have made a big quiche here, but, if you don't eat it all, you can freeze what's left.

Serves 8–10 Preparation time 15 minutes: Cooking time about 50 minutes: Freezes well

Pastry
225 g (8 oz) plain flour
100 g (4 oz) butter, cut into dice
1 egg
2–3 tablespoons cold water
Filling
175 g (6 oz) baby spinach, washed and stalks removed
salt and pepper
100 g (4 oz) Stilton cheese, coarsely grated

100 g (4 oz) mature Cheddar cheese, coarsely grated
100 g (4 oz) red Leicester cheese, coarsely grated
100 g (4 oz) soft goat's cheese
5 eggs
600 ml (1 pint) double cream
2 tablespoons Dijon mustard

Preheat the oven to 190°C/375°F/Gas 5, and preheat a baking sheet to get very hot.

For the pastry, measure the flour and butter into a processor and whizz until you have fine breadcrumbs. Add the egg and water and whizz again until it forms a dough (you can, of course, do this by hand). Cover in clingfilm and rest in the fridge if time allows.

Roll out the pastry thinly and use it to line a deep 30 cm (12 in) loose-bottomed metal flan tin, making a lip around the edge. Prick the base all over with a fork.

To make the filling, stir-fry the spinach in a large non-stick frying pan over a high heat until just wilted; if there is any liquid in the pan, drain it off. Season the spinach with salt and pepper and spoon over the base of the pastry case. Arrange half of each cheese over the spinach. Beat the eggs, cream and mustard together in a bowl and season with salt and pepper. Pour this custard into the pastry case and sprinkle over the remaining cheese.

Carefully slide the flan tin on to the hot baking sheet in the oven and bake for 45–50 minutes until the pastry is cooked and the quiche is set and golden brown. Check after 25 minutes; if the top is getting too brown, cover with a piece of foil.

Serve hot with a dressed herby salad.

To cook in the Aga Slide the quiche directly on to the floor of the roasting oven for about 40 minutes until the pastry and top of the quiche are golden brown. After about 30 minutes, when the top is golden brown, you may need to slide the cold sheet on to the second set of runners.

Tip It is usual to 'bake blind' in a conventional oven, but this pastry is very thin, and I have preheated the baking sheet to very hot, which helps the pastry cook quickly and become crisp underneath. If you only have a thick china dish in which to make the quiche, line the pastry case with greaseproof paper, use baking beans or rice to weight it down, and 'bake blind' in the preheated oven for 15 minutes. Carefully remove the beans and paper and return the pastry to the oven for a further 5 minutes to dry out the pastry. Add the filling and continue as above.

Honey-roasted Butternut Squash Risotto

Risotto is real comfort food, and is best served as it is with shavings of Parmesan and nothing else. You could use pumpkin instead of the squash if you prefer. Lovely Lucinda, who helps us, adores this recipe, and always took it home when we tested it.

Serves 4–6 Preparation time 20 minutes: Cooking time 30 minutes: Not suitable for freezing

900 g (2 lb) butternut squash
3 tablespoons olive oil
salt and pepper
1 teaspoon runny honey
1 onion, roughly chopped
2 sticks celery, cut into 1 cm ($^1/_2$ in) cubes
1 x 2.5 cm (1 in) piece fresh ginger root, peeled and finely grated

225 g (8 oz) risotto rice
150 ml (5 fl oz) white wine
850 ml (1$^1/_2$ pints) boiling Vegetable Stock (see page 184)
juice of $^1/_2$ lemon
a small bunch of fresh flat-leaf parsley, chopped

Preheat the oven to 220°C/425°F/Gas 7.

Peel the squash, cut it in half lengthways, scoop out the seeds and discard them. Cut the squash flesh into 1 cm ($^1/_2$ in) even cubes, and transfer to a large roasting tin in a single layer. Pour over 2 tablespoons of the oil, season with salt and pepper, and toss so all the squash is covered with oil. Roast in the preheated oven for about 10–15 minutes. Pour over the honey and return to the oven for a further 10–15 minutes until golden brown and crisp.

Meanwhile make the risotto. Heat the remaining oil in a large non-stick frying pan. Add the onion, celery and ginger, and fry for a couple of minutes over a high heat. Lower the heat, cover and simmer for about 10 minutes. Remove the lid, and add the rice and wine. Stirring continuously, gradually add the boiling stock. Cover and cook until nearly all the liquid has been absorbed, stirring occasionally.

After about 20 minutes, when the rice is cooked, add the roasted squash and lemon juice, and season to taste. Sprinkle in the chopped parsley and serve immediately.

To cook in the Aga Roast the oiled and seasoned squash in a roasting tin on the floor of the roasting oven for about 20 minutes, pouring over the honey

continued next page

---

a secret from our kitchen

Often we have leftover food in our kitchen so for a change it is lovely to make a variation of a recipe. This one, for example, is a perfect way of using up leftover risotto. Shape the cold mixture into small balls, and insert a 1 cm ($^1/_2$ in) piece of Cheddar into the middle of each ball. Coat in a few breadcrumbs and fry in hot oil over a high heat for about 2 minutes on each side until golden brown.

halfway through. Cook the onion, celery and ginger, covered, in the simmering oven for about 20 minutes. Remove the lid, and return the pan to the boiling plate. Add the rice and wine, and gradually add the boiling stock. Cover, and transfer to the simmering oven for about 25 minutes, stirring once during this time. Bring back to the boil on the boiling plate, then add the squash, lemon juice and seasoning to taste.

Tip Butternut squashes are tough to cut when raw, so use a strong sharp knife rather than a potato peeler. I find it easier to cut them into quarters and then remove the skin.

ⓥ Chunky Vegetable Tagine

The word 'tagine' is Moroccan, and is the name of both the stew and the dish that it is cooked in. Because most of us do not have a tagine dish, I cook this recipe in a deep frying pan with a lid. Traditionally, a tagine is made with diced lamb, and always has apricots in it, so this is my vegetarian version. With its subtle Moroccan spices, it has enormous depth of flavour, and is dark and rich in colour. The sweet potato and parsnips make it extra chunky.

Serves 4–6 Preparation time 10 minutes: Cooking time 40 minutes: Freezes well

2 tablespoons sunflower oil

1 large onion, sliced into large wedges

2 cloves garlic, crushed

1 green chilli, deseeded and finely chopped

2 teaspoons ground coriander

2 teaspoons ground cumin

1 teaspoon ground cinnamon

$1/2$ teaspoon ground turmeric

350 g (12 oz) sweet potato, peeled and chopped into 5 cm (2 in) cubes

350 g (12 oz) parsnips, peeled and chopped into 5 cm (2 in) cubes

300 ml (10 fl oz) Vegetable Stock (see page 184)

2 x 400 g cans chopped tomatoes

2 tablespoons runny honey

juice of $1/2$ lemon

50 g (2 oz) dried ready-to-eat apricots, halved

225 g (8 oz) cauliflower, cut into small florets

salt and pepper

chopped fresh parsley, to garnish

Heat the oil in a large non-stick frying pan. Add the onion, garlic and chilli, and fry over a high heat for a few minutes. Add the spices and fry for a few minutes more. Add the sweet potato and parsnips, stirring to coat them in the spices.

Stir in the stock, along with the remaining ingredients, except for the cauliflower, bring to the boil, and season with salt and pepper. Cover with a lid and simmer over a medium heat for about 10 minutes.

Add the cauliflower and continue to simmer for another 20–30 minutes or until all the vegetables are cooked. Serve with couscous (see page 55) and garnish with fresh parsley.

To cook in the Aga Fry and bring the mixture to the boil on the boiling plate. Cover with a lid, then transfer to the simmering oven for about 15 minutes. Bring back to the boil on the boiling plate, add the cauliflower and return to the simmering oven for a further 20–25 minutes or until all the vegetables are cooked.

Tip I find green chillies really 'lift' a recipe. They are milder than red ones, which makes the flavour subtle, and friends who are not keen on chillies don't even notice their inclusion in a recipe. The dried apricots you can buy now are mostly 'ready-to-eat', and do not need soaking ahead (as they used to). They are a very useful ingredient for both sweet and savoury dishes.

Braised Red Cabbage with Beetroot and Cranberries

Red cabbage reminds me of Christmas time, and its colour here is enhanced by that of the beetroot, the red wine and the traditionally Christmassy cranberries. This is a great dish to serve with game or any winter casserole – perfect with the Royal Berkshire Game Pie on page 68, for instance.

Serves 4–6 Preparation time 10 minutes: Cooking time about an hour: Freezes well

900 g (2 lb) red cabbage
100 g (4 oz) soft brown sugar
225 ml (8 fl oz) red wine
4 tablespoons red or white wine vinegar

225 g (8 oz) cooked beetroot, cut into walnut-sized pieces
75 g (3 oz) dried cranberries
salt and pepper

Cut the red cabbage into quarters, discard the core and slice thinly. Tip into a deep saucepan, add the sugar, wine and vinegar, and bring to the boil. Cover and simmer over a low heat for about 30 minutes.

Add the beetroot and cranberries to the saucepan, season with salt and pepper, and continue to cook, covered, over a low heat for a further 20–25 minutes or until the cabbage is tender and all the liquid has been absorbed.

Serve hot.

To cook in the Aga Bring the cabbage, sugar, wine and vinegar to the boil on the boiling plate, cover and transfer to the simmering oven for about 30 minutes. Add the beetroot, cranberries, salt and pepper, and bring back to the boil. Cover and return to the simmering oven for a further 30–35 minutes until the cabbage is tender and all the liquid has been absorbed.

Tip If you are using a small-based pan, all the liquid may not be absorbed. If this happens, remove the cabbage to a serving dish using a slotted spoon, boil the remaining liquid to reduce it, and pour over the cabbage. If you are not keen on cranberries, you can replace them with the same quantity of sultanas. Dried cranberries used to be only available at Christmas, but you can now buy them all year round.

a secret from our kitchen

Never cook red cabbage in an aluminium pan as it causes a reaction that makes the cabbage taste of metal.

Roasted Sweet Potatoes with Orange, Chilli and Coriander

V

I love sweet potatoes, but I think they are a vegetable in their own right and not a replacement for white potatoes. I often serve roasted sweet and white potatoes with my roasts, a delicious and unusual combination. This recipe is also perfect on the barbecue.

Serves 4–6 Preparation time 10 minutes: Cooking time about 30 minutes: Not suitable for freezing

3 large sweet potatoes, peeled and sliced into 2.5 cm (1 in) wedges

3 tablespoons olive oil

salt and pepper

1 small red chilli, deseeded and finely chopped

1 x 2.5 cm (1 in) piece fresh root ginger, peeled and finely chopped

finely grated zest of $\frac{1}{2}$ orange

2 small spring onions, finely sliced

2 tablespoons fresh coriander, chopped

Preheat the oven to 200°C/400°F/Gas 6.

Toss the potato wedges in 2 tablespoons of the oil and season with salt and pepper. Arrange in a single layer in a greased roasting tin or on a baking sheet.

Slide into the preheated oven and roast for about 15 minutes or until golden brown. Turn the wedges over and return to the oven for a further 15 minutes or until the potatoes are cooked through.

Add the chilli, ginger, orange zest, spring onions and remaining olive oil to the potatoes and return to the hot oven for about 5 minutes.

Just before serving, sprinkle over the coriander. Serve hot.

To cook in the Aga Slide the roasting tin directly on to the floor of the roasting oven for about 15 minutes. Turn the potatoes over and return to the floor of the roasting oven for a further 15 minutes until the potatoes are tender. Sprinkle over the chilli, ginger, orange and spring onions and return to floor of the roasting oven for about 5 minutes.

Tip If you want to cook this on the barbecue, wrap the oiled and seasoned potatoes in foil and sit on the hot coals for about 30 minutes until the potatoes are tender. Sprinkle over the flavourings, re-wrap in the same foil, and return to the coals for about 5 minutes.

a secret from our kitchen

I have often made these as a nibble for a party – serve as above on a platter with a bowl of soured cream to dip into. They are fine to eat with your hands or a cocktail stick. You can also make this recipe with butternut squash or pumpkin if liked.

Creamy Celeriac Purée

This is a super alternative to mashed potatoes or mashed swede, with its subtle celery flavour. It can be served with winter casseroles, venison, beef or the game pie on page 68. It can also be made ahead and reheated, so is perfect if you are cooking for lots of people.

Serves 8 Preparation time 10 minutes: Cooking time 30 minutes: Not suitable for freezing

1.8 kg (4 lb) celeriac
salt and pepper
1 x 200 ml carton full-fat crème fraîche

2 tablespoons fresh chives, snipped
butter if necessary

Peel the celeriac with a knife and cut into even-sized chunks of about 2.5 cm (1 in). Boil in salted water for about 20–25 minutes until really soft but not waterlogged. Drain well.

Carefully tip into the processor with the crème fraîche, and season with salt and pepper. Blend until really smooth. Stir in the chives and serve immediately.

If you want to serve it later, cool the purée (before adding the chives), then turn it into a buttered ovenproof dish, cover with clingfilm and keep in the fridge until needed. To reheat, slide the dish, covered with foil, into the oven preheated to 180°C/350°F/Gas 4 for about 30 minutes until piping hot. Stir in the chives.

To cook in the Aga Bring the celeriac chunks to the boil in boiling salted water on the boiling plate. Drain, cover with a lid and transfer to the simmering oven for about 50 minutes until really soft and tender. Follow as above. To reheat, slide the dish, covered in foil, into the simmering oven for about an hour.

Tip It is very important to cook the celeriac until really tender, otherwise you will have a lumpy purée.

Herby Parsnip and Potato Cakes Ⓥ

Potato cakes are great to serve with many different dishes. The parsnip used here gives texture (as well as flavour), so they are not totally smooth as most potato cakes are.

Makes 6 cakes Preparation time 15 minutes: Cooking time 5 minutes: Not suitable for freezing

350 g (12 oz) potatoes
350 g (12 oz) parsnips
15 g (^{1}/$_2$ oz) butter
1 tablespoon chopped fresh parsley

1 tablespoon chopped fresh thyme
salt and pepper
a little plain flour
2 tablespoons sunflower oil

Peel the potatoes and parsnips and cut into even-sized cubes. Boil in salted water until tender (this depends on their size). Drain.

Mash the vegetables together with the butter and herbs, and season with salt and pepper. Set aside to cool.

Using your hands, shape into six flat round cakes about 2.5 cm (1 in) deep. Dust a little flour all over the cakes.

Heat the oil in a wide frying pan and fry the cakes over a high heat for about 5 minutes on both sides until golden brown and hot in the middle. Serve immediately.

To cook in the Aga Fry the cakes in a large non-stick frying pan on the boiling plate.

Tip These cakes can be made and fried up to 12 hours in ahead and reheated in a moderate oven until piping hot.

a secret from our kitchen

Mary's herb garden is just wonderful, and I feel so lucky to have such a selection of fresh luscious herbs outside the kitchen door. Parsley is the most useful, and it is best sown from seed in the spring and again in late summer. To produce the finest crop, pour boiling water along the drill and scatter the seeds on top. Cover with a layer of tilth or John Innes No 2. Cover with a cloche to maintain a winter supply.

pasta
and
stir-fries

Saturday Night Spag Bol

I know everyone has their own way of making spaghetti bolognese, but you don't often see the recipe in cookery books – so this is for those of you who would like to try a different one. There are many, many variations, and I'm sure the Italians would have something to say about mine, but my friends love it!

Serves 6 Preparation time 15 minutes: Cooking time 1 1/2 hours: Meat sauce freezes well

a secret from our kitchen

The redcurrant jelly brings together the flavours, especially when using tomatoes, as they can be slightly bitter. If you do not have any redcurrant jelly in the cupboard, use an alternative fruit jelly or some mango chutney.

350 g (12 oz) spaghetti
freshly grated Parmesan, to serve
Sauce
900 g (2 lb) minced beef
1 large Spanish onion, thinly sliced
2 cloves garlic, crushed
225 g (8 oz) cup mushrooms, sliced
2 heaped tablespoons plain flour

150 ml (5 fl oz) red wine
150 ml (5 fl oz) Beef Stock (see page 184)
1 x 500 g carton tomato passata
1 x 400 g can chopped tomatoes
2 tablespoons tomato purée
2 tablespoons redcurrant jelly
1–2 tablespoons Worcestershire sauce
2 tablespoons chopped fresh thyme

Brown the mince in a large non-stick frying pan over a high heat – in its natural fat – stirring until completely brown. Add the onion, garlic and mushrooms, and fry for a further 5 minutes. Sprinkle in the flour, then blend in the wine, stock, passata and tomatoes, and stir over a high heat. Bring to the boil, add the rest of the ingredients, boil for a further 5 minutes, then cover with a lid, lower the heat and simmer for about 1$^1/_2$ hours until the meat is tender.

Cook the spaghetti in boiling salted water according to the packet instructions. Serve the drained spaghetti in bowls with a spoonful or two of the sauce on top.

Serve with freshly grated Parmesan.

To cook in the Aga Brown the mince in a large non-stick frying pan on the boiling plate, stirring until brown all over. Continue as above. Cook the sauce, covered, in the simmering oven for about 1$^1/_2$–2 hours until tender.

Tip I like to brown the mince ahead, which seals in the juices, retains the flavour and gives a lovely colour to the mince. The long slow cooking time gives a full flavour to the meat and tenderises it – quick cooking can make it tough. Buy the best mince you can, as your sauce will only be as good as the mince you buy.

Double Mushroom and Garlic Tagliatelle

Ⓥ

We have such a super choice of mushrooms available to us now, because so many more types of mushroom are being cultivated – button, cap, flat, portobella, chestnut, oyster, shiitake, the list goes on. You can choose whichever mushroom you prefer, but be sure to use firm ones (i.e. chestnut, button or cap).

Serves 6 Preparation time 10 minutes: Cooking time 10 minutes: Not suitable for freezing

1 tablespoon olive oil

225 g (8 oz) chestnut mushrooms, sliced

150 g (5 oz) oyster mushrooms, sliced

2 fat cloves garlic, crushed

1 x 200 ml tub full-fat crème fraîche

25 g (1 oz) Parmesan cheese, freshly grated

salt and pepper

350 g (12 oz) dried tagliatelle pasta

175 g (6 oz) firm cherry tomatoes, halved

4 good tablespoons chopped fresh parsley

extra shavings of Parmesan, to garnish

a secret from our kitchen

The best way to make shavings of Parmesan is to buy fresh Parmesan in a block and, using a potato peeler, shave from the flat side.

Heat the oil in a large non-stick frying pan, add the mushrooms and garlic, and fry for a few minutes until just starting to colour. Pour in the crème fraîche and boil over a high heat for a few minutes so it reduces a little. Add the grated Parmesan and some salt and pepper.

Boil the pasta in boiling salted water according to packet instructions until al dente (about 10 minutes).

Drain the pasta well, and add to the pan with the mushrooms. Stir so all the pasta is coated. Just before serving, stir in the cherry tomatoes and parsley. Turn into a hot serving dish and sprinkle shavings of Parmesan over the top.

To cook in the Aga Cook in a large non-stick frying pan on the boiling plate.

Tip It is important to use full-fat crème fraîche as the low-fat version has too much water in it and will make the sauce too runny. Using full-fat crème fraîche still makes a thinner sauce than double cream, which is why I have added Parmesan, to thicken the sauce a little. You can use the same amount of double cream if preferred.

Spaghetti Veneto

Ⓥ

This recipe is full of wonderful flavours with a huge Italian influence. We are so lucky with the new ingredients widely available to us from different countries in our supermarkets and farmers' markets. Pine nuts and sun-blushed tomatoes are such a joy to use, giving texture and flavour. If you are doubling this recipe you can make the cheese paste in a processor, if preferred.

Serves 4–6 Preparation time 10 minutes: Cooking time 12 minutes: Not suitable for freezing

a secret from our kitchen

Mary and I invented this for one of our workshop days. We had big debates about which pasta to use – Mary likes penne but I prefer spaghetti. You can, of course, use whichever you like as both are delicious! Either way, it's very popular and looks stunning too!

50 g (2 oz) pine nuts
250 g (9 oz) baby spinach, washed and
    coarsely chopped
150 g (5 oz) Dolcelatte cheese
1–2 cloves garlic, crushed
150 ml (5 fl oz) single cream

225 g (8 oz) sun-blushed tomatoes,
    coarsely chopped
350 g (12 oz) spaghetti
salt and pepper
freshly grated nutmeg

Dry-fry the pine nuts in a non-stick frying pan until golden all over – watch them like a hawk! Set aside and keep warm.

Wilt the spinach in a large non-stick frying pan over a high heat. Mash the cheese and garlic together in a bowl and gradually mix in the cream to make a paste, until just blended. Add the cheese paste and sun-blushed tomatoes to the spinach and stir until hot.

Boil the spaghetti in a large pan of salted water until just tender, about 10 minutes, or according to the instructions on the packet. Drain well.

Add the spaghetti to the frying pan and stir briefly over a high heat. Season with black pepper and nutmeg, then turn into a warmed serving dish. Sprinkle the warm pine nuts over the top and serve at once.

To cook in the Aga Fry in a large non-stick frying pan on the boiling plate. Boil the spaghetti in salted boiling water on the boiling plate.

Tip Sun-blushed tomatoes are a huge improvement on the sun-dried ones – the colour, texture and flavour are all better. In different supermarkets they are called different things – sun-ripened, half-blushed, sun-softened – but they are all similar.

Penne with Caramelised Onions, Crab and Capers

A fresh pasta dish which is low in fat and perfect for throwing together after a hard day's work. All the ingredients can be bought in the supermarket, it only takes a few minutes to cook, and it is so full of flavour that I have served it at a dinner party. If you prefer, you can use fusilli pasta instead of penne.

Serves 4–6 Preparation time 5 minutes: Cooking time 10 minutes: Not suitable for freezing

225 g (8 oz) dried penne pasta
salt and pepper
3 tablespoons olive oil
1/2 onion, thinly sliced
2 cloves garlic, crushed
2 x 175 g cans white crab meat, drained

3 tablespoons capers from a jar, rinsed and drained
juice of 1 lemon
25 g (1 oz) pitted black olives, halved
4 good tablespoons chopped fresh parsley

Cook the pasta in a pan of salted boiling water for about 12 minutes or according to packet instructions. Drain.

Meanwhile, to make the sauce, heat the oil in a large non-stick frying pan, add the onion and garlic, and fry over a high heat for about 5 minutes, stirring, until golden brown. Add the crab meat, capers and lemon juice. Lower the heat and simmer over a low heat for about 5 minutes.

Stir in the olives, cooked pasta and parsley and season with salt and pepper. Serve immediately.

To cook in the Aga Cook both the pasta and sauce on the boiling plate, stirring.

Tip White crab meat in cans is excellent. I think John West is the best. Drain well and season well with salt and pepper as this brings out the flavour.

Egg Noodle Stir-fry with Black Bean Sauce (V)

This stir-fry is very healthy, and it's vegetarian too. It may seem a bit of a cheat using bottled sauce, but many of them are very good, and the end result is delicious.

Serves 4–6 Preparation time 10 minutes: Cooking time 10 minutes: Not suitable for freezing

175 g (6 oz) medium egg noodles
150 g (5 oz) baby sweetcorn, sliced in half
   lengthways
1 tablespoon sunflower oil
1 large leek, halved lengthways and cut
   into long strips

1 large courgette, sliced into thin batons
1 large carrot, coarsely grated
8 tablespoons black bean sauce
2 tablespoons white wine or rice vinegar
2 tablespoons soy sauce
25 g (1 oz) salted peanuts

Cook the noodles according to the packet instructions until al dente. Cook the baby corn in with the noodles for about 3 minutes. Drain both, and refresh in cold water.

Heat the oil in large non-stick frying pan. Add the leek and courgette and fry for a minute or so, then add the carrot and remaining ingredients, except for the peanuts.

Stir in the noodles so they are coated in the sauce and mixed with the vegetables. Heat briefly together, then turn into a serving dish and sprinkle with the peanuts.

To cook in the Aga Cook the noodles in boiling salted water on the boiling plate, according to packet instructions. Stir-fry on the boiling plate in large wide-based non-stick pan.

Tip Keep the skin on the courgette. This helps the pieces to keep their shape, and the bright green and pale green-yellow together look lovely too.

a secret from our kitchen

When stir-frying on the Aga, use a wide-based pan so that it covers as much of the Aga plate as possible. A wok is not ideal on the Aga as the base is small, and therefore heat is lost around the sides of the wok.

Stir-fried Chicken with Sweet Pepper and Creamy Basil Sauce

Stir-fries don't usually have a creamy sauce, but I think this is nice for a change. This is a perfect recipe for supper with friends after work.

Serves 4–6 Preparation time 10 minutes: Cooking time 10 minutes: Not suitable for freezing

4 chicken breasts, boneless and skinless
1 tablespoon sunflower oil
2 yellow peppers, deseeded and thinly sliced
225 g (8 oz) chestnut mushrooms, halved
225 g (8 oz) baby leaf greens, very thinly sliced

150 ml (5 fl oz) pouring double cream
3 teaspoons red or green pesto
75 g (3 oz) peppadew peppers from a jar, halved
salt and pepper
2 tablespoons fresh basil leaves

Slice the chicken breasts into long thin strips. Heat the oil in a large non-stick frying pan, and cook the chicken strips over a high heat until golden brown all over and cooked through. Remove from the frying pan using a slotted spoon and set aside.

Add the peppers, mushrooms and baby leaf greens to the pan, and fry over a high heat for a few minutes. Mix together the cream and pesto in a small bowl, then add to the pan with the peppadew peppers and some salt and pepper.

Return the chicken to the pan and stir-fry briefly to heat through. Garnish with basil leaves and serve immediately with egg noodles, rice or crusty bread.

Tip Peppadews are baby sweet peppers from South Africa. They are sold in a jar in all good supermarkets near the olives and gherkins. Alternatively, you could add cherry tomatoes. Baby leaf greens are sold in all good supermarkets and farmers' markets, and are the greens I used to give to my rabbits when I was little! They are delicious, to human and rabbit alike, but if you can't find them, use fresh spinach instead.

Colourful Pork and Vegetable Stir-fry

This stir-fry is very healthy, and pretty to look at as well. I love including cashew nuts – just the salted ones – in stir-fries, as they add such flavour and crunch. Pak-choi is a modern Chinese vegetable, and one I love. The white part has crunch and the top end, the green part, is a little like spinach. I think it is best stir-fried, but it can be griddled to serve as a vegetable on its own.

Serves 4–6 Preparation time 10 minutes: Cooking time 10 minutes: Not suitable for freezing

1 tablespoon olive oil

225 g (8 oz) pork fillet, sliced into long strips

3 tablespoons runny honey

3 large spring onions, sliced on the diagonal

1 red pepper, deseeded and thinly sliced

5 sticks celery, thinly sliced on the diagonal

2 cloves garlic, crushed

225 g (8 oz) pak-choi, sliced coarsely, white and green parts kept separate

4 tablespoons white wine vinegar

4 tablespoons soy sauce

1 x 227 g can pineapple rings, drained and chopped into chunks

50 g (2 oz) salted cashew nuts

salt and pepper

a secret from our kitchen

Did you know that half of all men don't like celery? A sweeping statement, I know, but this is what I've learned from our demonstrations. If we have celery in a recipe, half the audience will say that their 'other halves' don't like it! If this is the case with you and yours, replace the celery with one large leek, sliced.

Heat the oil in a large non-stick frying pan or wok over a high heat. Add the pork to the pan and pour over 1 tablespoon of the honey. Fry for 2–3 minutes until just cooked and brown. Remove with a slotted spoon and set aside.

Add the spring onions, pepper, celery, garlic and the white parts of the pak-choi to the frying pan, and stir for a further 3 minutes. Add the vinegar, soy sauce and the remaining 2 tablespoons of honey. Bring to the boil, and reduce for a few minutes.

Return the pork to the pan, add the green parts of the pak-choi, the pineapple and cashew nuts, and season with salt and pepper. Stir-fry for a moment or two to heat through. Serve hot with noodles or rice, or on its own.

To cook in the Aga Fry in a large non-stick frying pan or wok on the boiling plate.

Tip Adding honey to the pork when stir-frying makes it brown very quickly and adds to the flavour too.

one-dish

oven bakes

Quick Haddock and Rocket Bake

This fish bake is very quick to do, and I think it is perfect for Christmas Eve or for a casual supper with friends. Leaving the haddock in large pieces gives texture to the dish. I invented this recipe in a hurry, and it is now one of my favourites. Serve with mash or crusty bread.

Serves 6–8 Preparation time 10 minutes: Cooking time 20–25 minutes: Not suitable for freezing

40 g (1 1/2 oz) butter

2 cloves garlic, crushed

5 large tomatoes, sliced into 1 cm (1/2 in) thick slices

350 g (12 oz) red peppers from a jar, cut into large slices

2 x 50 g bags fresh rocket

salt and pepper

900 g (2 lb) fresh haddock fillet, skinned

150 ml (5 fl oz) double cream

75 g (3 oz) Parmesan cheese, freshly grated

paprika

Preheat the oven to 180°C/350°F/Gas 4. You will need a lightly buttered 1.2 litre (2 pint) fairly shallow ovenproof dish.

Melt the butter in a large non-stick frying pan. Add the garlic and arrange the tomato slices flat in a single layer in the pan. Fry the slices for a minute on each side. Remove with a fish slice and set aside. Toss the peppers in the pan for a minute, then transfer with the garlic and butter to the plate with the tomatoes.

Empty the bags of rocket into the base of the buttered ovenproof dish, and season with salt and pepper. Arrange the tomatoes and peppers over the top of the rocket. Cut the haddock fillets into six thick strips and arrange over the tomatoes and peppers. Season with pepper. Pour the cream over the top of the haddock, season and sprinkle over the cheese. Dust with paprika.

Bake in the preheated oven for about 20 minutes until the fish is cooked and golden brown on top. Serve hot.

To cook in the Aga Fry the tomatoes and peppers as above in a non-stick frying pan on the boiling plate. Slide the dish on to the second set of runners in the roasting oven for about 20 minutes until the fish is cooked and the topping is golden brown.

Tip I have used peppers from a jar as it is easier than cooking fresh peppers. Buy peppers in oil rather than in brine, as they have a much better flavour. You can, of course, use fresh peppers if you have an abundance of them: halve, remove the seeds and grill until the skin is black, then skin and chop into large slices before frying in the garlic butter.

Mexican Tuna Pasta Bake

A quick recipe for the family, which can be made ahead. If your family does not like chilli, then you can leave it out. I use a red chilli, but you could use a green one, which is milder.

Serves 6 Preparation time 20 minutes: Cooking time 20 minutes: Not suitable for freezing

225 g (8 oz) penne pasta
salt and pepper
1 tablespoon olive oil
2 green peppers, deseeded and chopped
   into 1 cm ($^1/_2$ in) dice
1 red chilli, deseeded and finely chopped

2 x 400 g cans chopped tomatoes
juice of $^1/_2$ lime
1 x 400 g can tuna chunks in oil, drained
100 g (4 oz) feta cheese, crumbled
150ml (5 fl oz) soured cream

a secret from our kitchen

Warming a lemon or lime helps to get more juice from it. Just heat the whole fruit in the microwave for 30 seconds, or in the simmering oven of the Aga for 10 minutes.

Preheat the oven to 180°C/350°F/Gas 4. You will need a 1 litre ($1^3/_4$ pint) ovenproof dish.

Cook the pasta in boiling salted water according to packet instructions until al dente, then drain and refresh in cold water while making the sauce.

Heat the oil in a large non-stick frying pan. Add the peppers and chilli and fry over a high heat for about 3 minutes. Pour in the chopped tomatoes, cover and simmer over low heat for about 15 minutes until the peppers are just soft.

Stir in the cooked pasta and lime juice. Carefully mix in the tuna chunks (try to keep the chunks as whole as possible), and season with salt and pepper. Spoon into the ovenproof dish and sprinkle the feta and dollop the soured cream over the top.

Bake in the preheated oven for about 15–20 minutes until piping hot.

To cook in the Aga Slide the dish on to the second set of runners in the roasting oven for about 15–20 minutes until piping hot.

Tip Be sure to buy tuna chunks, and be careful when mixing in with the tomato mixture not to break the chunks up too much. If you cannot buy soured cream, use full-fat crème fraîche instead.

Broccoli and Cauliflower Cheese with Crispy Bacon

This is a colourful variation on classic cauliflower cheese. For vegetarians, leave out the bacon – it will be just as delicious.

Serves 4–6 Preparation time 10–15 minutes: Cooking time 20 minutes (or under the grill, for about 10 minutes, see the Tip): Not suitable for freezing

150 g (5 oz) streaky bacon
350 g (12 oz) cauliflower florets
salt and pepper
225 g (8 oz) small broccoli florets
Sauce
50 g (2 oz) butter
50 g (2 oz) plain flour

600 ml (1 pint) full-fat milk
50 g (2 oz) Parmesan cheese, freshly grated
100 g (4 oz) mature Cheddar cheese, grated
1 rounded teaspoon Dijon mustard

a secret from our kitchen

We always buy dry-cured bacon. Because of the dry-curing, there is a lot less water to come out of the bacon, and it therefore crisps quicker while retaining its flavour.

Preheat the oven to 200°C/400°F/Gas 6. You will need a deep 1.5 litre (2³/₄ pint) ovenproof dish.

Snip the bacon into thin strips and fry in a non-stick frying pan until crisp. Set aside.

Cook the cauliflower florets in boiling salted water for about 5 minutes. Add the broccoli and boil for a further 3 minutes. Drain and refresh in cold water (this stops the cooking and sets the bright green colour of the broccoli). Pile the vegetables into the ovenproof dish and sprinkle over the crisp bacon.

To make the sauce, melt the butter over a high heat, then off the heat blend in the flour to make a roux. Return the pan to the heat and gradually add in the milk, whisking all the time until the sauce thickens and is smooth. Add 25 g (1 oz) of the Parmesan and 75 g (3 oz) of the Cheddar to the sauce with the mustard and some salt and pepper.

Pour the sauce over the vegetables and bacon in the dish, and sprinkle with the remaining cheeses. Bake in the preheated oven for about 20 minutes until piping hot and golden brown.

To cook in the Aga Fry the bacon in a non-stick frying pan on the boiling plate until crisp. Cook the vegetables as above on the boiling plate. Slide the prepared dish on to the top set of runners in the roasting oven and bake for about 20 minutes until piping hot and golden brown.

continued next page

Tip If refreshing vegetables, do not leave them sitting in water, as they will soak up the water and become soggy. Rinse them under cold water until stone cold and set aside in a colander. If serving immediately, do not refresh the vegetables in cold water. Make the sauce first, then cook the vegetables until just tender, drain, pour over the hot sauce, sprinkle with cheese and pop under the grill for about 10 minutes, or until golden brown and bubbling. Florets are the flower tops of broccoli and cauliflower. I also love the broccoli stalks, which you can use as well as the florets. Peel them, cut into thin strips, and cook them with the cauliflower and broccoli florets.

Leek and Ham Gratin Blankets

In the autumn when your home-grown leeks are at their finest, this recipe is perfect. Trim freshly dug leeks and wash well – home-grown ones are always full of earth. Try to use smallish leeks, as large leeks can be a little tough for this recipe.

Serves 4 Preparation time 10–15 minutes; Cooking time about 20–30 minutes: Not suitable for freezing

4 small thin leeks, about 25 cm
  (10 in) long
salt and pepper
4 large thin slices good-quality lean ham
a little grainy mustard
25 g (1 oz) mature Cheddar cheese, grated
25 g (1 oz) fresh breadcrumbs
paprika

Cheese sauce
40g (1 1/2 oz) butter
40g (1 1/2 oz) plain flour
450 ml (15 fl oz) milk
1 teaspoon Dijon mustard
70 g (2 1/2 oz) mature Cheddar cheese, grated

Preheat the oven to 200°C/400°F/Gas 6.

Slice the leeks in half widthways so you have eight pieces. Cook in a pan of boiling salted water for about 4–5 minutes (or a few minutes longer if they are fat leeks) until just tender. Drain and refresh in cold water. Dry and cut each piece of leek into three.

Slice each piece of ham in half then spread one side with a little grainy mustard. Arrange three slices of each leek end to end on top of each piece of ham (mustard side touching the leek). Roll the ham around the leek so it goes back into a leek shape. Arrange in a single layer in a shallow ovenproof dish.

To make the cheese sauce, melt the butter in a small saucepan, remove from the heat, add the flour and whisk to form a roux. Return to the heat and gradually whisk in the milk until smooth. Bring to the boil and continue whisking until the sauce has thickened and is smooth. Add the mustard, cheese and salt and pepper.

Pour the cheese sauce over the leeks and ham in the dish. Sprinkle over the cheese and breadcrumbs. Bake in the preheated oven for about 20–30 minutes or until hot in the middle and golden brown and crisp on top. Sprinkle with a little paprika.

To cook in the Aga Cook the leeks in boiling salted water on the boiling plate for about 4 minutes until just tender. Bake the dish on the highest set of runners in the roasting oven for about 20–30 minutes until golden brown and crisp on top.

Tip This dish can be made completely up to 8 hours ahead, ready to go in the oven. Be sure to dry the leeks well before wrapping in the ham otherwise the dish will become wet. The leeks are much easier to eat if they are cut into smaller pieces before wrapping.

Carbonnade of Beef with Double Potato Topping

'Carbonnade' means a casserole of beef cooked in beer, and it is especially delicious served with winter veg. The mushrooms need to be quite chunky so they don't overcook when braising. If they are small, leave them whole.

Serves 6 Preparation time 15 minutes: Cooking time about 2 hours: Freezes well without the potato topping

3 tablespoons sunflower oil

900 g (2 lb) braising steak, diced

1 large red onion, sliced into chunky wedges

2 cloves garlic, crushed

225 g (8 oz) chestnut mushrooms, halved, or quartered if large

40 g (1½ oz) plain flour

300 ml (10 fl oz) lager

150ml (5 fl oz) Beef Stock (see page 184)

1 tablespoon tomato purée

1 tablespoon light brown sugar

175 g (6 oz) sun-dried tomatoes, each one snipped into four

salt and pepper

Topping

450 g (1 lb) sweet potatoes

450 g (1 lb) old potatoes

Heat 2 tablespoons of the oil in a large non-stick frying pan or casserole. Fry the meat over a high heat until browned all over (you may need to do this in batches). Remove the meat from the pan with a slotted spoon and set aside.

Add the remaining oil to the same pan, along with the onion, garlic and mushrooms, and fry over a high heat for few minutes. Return the meat to the pan, sprinkle in the flour, then gradually blend in the lager and stock, mixing continuously over a high heat until smooth. Bring to the boil, and add the remaining ingredients and salt and pepper. Cover, reduce the heat and cook at a simmer for about 1½ hours or until the meat is tender. Taste for seasoning and set aside to get completely cold.

For the topping, peel both lots of potatoes and cut into even-sized chunks. Cook in boiling salted water until tender, then drain and mash with salt and pepper to taste.

Once the casserole is cold, tip into a deep ovenproof dish of about 1.7 litre (3 pint) capacity (not too wide) and top with the potato topping. Bake in an oven preheated to 200°C/400°F/Gas 6 for about 30–40 minutes until piping hot.

To cook in the Aga Cook the casserole, covered, in the simmering oven for about 1½ hours until the meat is tender. Reheat the whole dish

continued next page

on the grid shelf on the floor of the roasting oven for about 30 minutes until piping hot.

Tip The casserole will seem quite thick before it is cooked, but, as it cooks, the juices from the onions and mushrooms will thin it down to the right consistency. If preferred, you can use skirt beef instead of braising or stewing steak. Unfortunately, it is not available in supermarkets, but all good local butchers sell it. It is a lovely cut of meat, especially good in steak and kidney pie

Lasagne with Aubergine and Mozzarella

I invented this dish for my father who loves both lasagne and aubergine – so I thought I would put the two together! To save time, it does not have a classic cheese sauce, just a very quick creamy sauce instead.

Serves 6 Preparation time 50 minutes: Cooking time 40 minutes: Freezes well

225 g (8 oz) (12 sheets) lasagne pasta
   (no need to pre-cook)
salt and pepper
175 g (6 oz) mozzarella cheese, grated
175 g (6 oz) mature Cheddar cheese,
   grated

Mince
700 g (1¹/₂ lb) minced beef
2 cloves garlic, crushed
1 large onion, chopped
225 g (8 oz) cup mushrooms, sliced
1 small aubergine, halved lengthways,
   then sliced finely widthways

2 tablespoons plain flour
2 x 400 g cans chopped tomatoes
150 ml (5 fl oz) red wine or port
2 tablespoons tomato purée
1 tablespoon redcurrant jelly
1 bay leaf

Cheese sauce
150 ml (5 fl oz) double cream
1 x 250 g tub ricotta cheese
1 teaspoon Dijon mustard

a secret from our kitchen

If you freeze a lot, it can be frustrating when the dish you want to use for the next recipe is already in the freezer. What we do is take the dish out of the freezer, run a knife round the edges, and set aside for about an hour. Tip the contents upside down (it will come out in a block), wrap in foil, label well (with the name of recipe and the dish it was frozen in), and return to the freezer. You then have the empty dish itself to use again. When you want to serve the original frozen recipe, simply remove from the freezer, unwrap from the foil, return to the same dish, defrost and cook.

Preheat the oven to 200°C/400°F/Gas 6. You will need a shallow ovenproof dish of about 2.2 litres (4 pints) capacity.

Fry the mince in a large non-stick frying pan over a high heat until brown (using the natural fat from the meat). Add the garlic, onion, mushrooms and aubergine, and continue to fry over a high heat for a few minutes. Sprinkle in the flour and stir until all the meat and vegetables are coated. Blend in the tomatoes, wine, tomato purée and redcurrant jelly. Stir continuously over a high heat for few minutes. Season with salt and pepper and add the bay leaf. Bring to the boil, cover and simmer over a low heat for about 40 minutes until tender.

To make the cheese sauce, mix together the cream, ricotta cheese and mustard. Season with salt and pepper.

Remove the bay leaf from the mince. Spoon a third of the mince into the base of the dish, cover with a third of the cheese sauce and sprinkle over a third of the grated cheeses. Arrange six sheets of pasta over the top. Repeat, using half of the remaining mince and cheese sauce, ending with the remaining six sheets of pasta, and finish with the remaining mince, sauce and grated cheeses on the top.

Cook in the preheated oven for about 40–50 minutes until the pasta is tender. Serve immediately with crusty bread and a crisp salad.

To cook in the Aga Cook the mince, covered, in the simmering oven for about 40 minutes. Bake the lasagne on the lowest set of runners in the roasting oven for about 40–50 minutes until golden brown and tender.

Tip I have not added any extra oil to this recipe – just the natural fat from the mince. If you use extra lean mince, you may need to add a little extra oil.

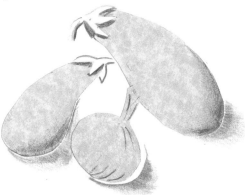

Roasted Vegetable Cannelloni

Ⓥ

It has become quite difficult to buy cannelloni tubes, so I have used fresh sheets of lasagne (you can also use dried, see below). This is a really good vegetarian dish that everyone can enjoy – and there is no white sauce to make! The basic tomato and basil sauce is a great stand-by to serve with all pasta, and it freezes well too.

Serves 6 Preparation time 20 minutes: Cooking time 1 hour: Not suitable for freezing

1 x 225 g (8 oz) fresh lasagne sheets (normally 12 sheets)
75 g (3 oz) Gruyère cheese, grated

Filling
1 large aubergine
2 courgettes
2 red peppers
2 large onions
2 tablespoons olive oil
2 fat cloves garlic, crushed
salt and pepper

2 tablespoons pesto from a jar
25 g (1 oz) Parmesan cheese, freshly grated

Tomato and basil sauce
1–2 tablespoons olive oil
1 large onion, finely chopped
2 fat cloves garlic, crushed
1 x 700g jar tomato passata
2 tablespoons chopped fresh basil
1 tablespoon balsamic vinegar
a little caster sugar to taste

Preheat the oven to 220°C/425°F/Gas 7. You will need a 1.2 litre (2 pint) shallow ovenproof dish.

First roast the vegetables for the filling. Chop the aubergine, courgettes, peppers and onions into tiny neat dice by hand. Coat the vegetables in the oil and mix with the garlic and some salt and pepper. Roast in a large roasting tin in the preheated oven for about 30 minutes until tender. Remove from the oven and mix in the pesto and Parmesan.

To make the tomato sauce, heat the oil, add the onion and garlic, and fry for about 2–3 minutes. Cover with a lid and cook over a low heat for about 15 minutes until tender. Turn up the heat and stir in the passata. Wash out the passata jar with about 150 ml (5 fl oz) water and add to the sauce. Season and bring to the boil, cover, lower the heat and cook for about 20 minutes. Add the basil and balsamic vinegar, and sugar if you like.

Follow the instructions on the packet of fresh lasagne: most say soak in boiling water for 5 minutes to soften. (For dried pasta, soak the sheets, a few at a time, for 15 minutes in boiling water until soft.) Lay the 12 lasagne sheets on the work surface, divide the vegetable filling between them and roll up tightly.

Pour half the tomato sauce into the chosen ovenproof dish so all the cannelloni can lie flat. Arrange the cannelloni on the sauce and spoon over the remaining sauce. Sprinkle over the cheese.

Turn down the oven to 200°C/400°F/Gas 6 and bake the cannelloni for about 30 minutes until piping hot.

To cook in the Aga Cook the vegetables in a large roasting tin on the floor of the roasting oven for about 25–30 minutes. Soften the onion for the sauce, covered, in the simmering oven for about 25 minutes. Bake the cannelloni on the second set of runners in the roasting oven for about 25–30 minutes.

Tip The vegetables must be diced up very small: this is what makes the cannelloni extra special. But don't be tempted to chop the onions in the processor, because the result would be too wet and lacking in texture.

Treacle-glazed Chicken

Perfect for the family, as it is both delicious, and very quick and easy. It has a small amount of sauce, but a lot of flavour. Serve with baby new potatoes or mash.

Serves 4 Preparation time 5 minutes: Cooking time 20 minutes: Not suitable for freezing

4 chicken breasts, boneless and skinless
salt and pepper
Sauce
2 tablespoons black treacle

2 tablespoons tomato ketchup
1 tablespoon redcurrant jelly
3 tablespoons orange juice

Preheat the oven to 180°C/350°F/Gas 4.

Arrange the chicken breasts snugly in a small roasting tin and season with salt and pepper. Mix together the sauce ingredients in a small bowl, season with salt and pepper, and pour over the chicken breasts.

Bake in the oven for about 20 minutes until the chicken is cooked. Serve hot.

To cook in the Aga Slide the roasting tin on to the second set of runners in the roasting oven for about 15–20 minutes until the chicken breasts are just tender.

Tip You do not need to use freshly squeezed orange juice – use the type that you have for breakfast. When a skinless chicken breast is cooked, it lacks the brown crispy top you get with a skin-on breast. Here, however, the glaze makes the breasts look very attractive, with a lovely brown shine.

outdoor
eating

Feta and Mint Salad with a Splash of Pomegranate (V) 128
Oriental Noodle Salad (V) 130
Fresh Salmon and Potato Salad with Herb Dressing 131
Thyme-marinated Prawns with a Squeeze of Lemon and Lime 132

Twisted Chicken and Courgette Spicy Kebabs 135
Fresh Mango Chicken with Watercress Salad 137
Sticky Spare Ribs 138
Quick Herby Pepperoni Scone Pizza with Double Cheese 139

Feta and Mint Salad with a splash of Pomegranate

This recipe is perfect as a salad in its own right or as an accompanying salad. I just use the pomegranate seeds, and not the juice, for this recipe.

Serves 4-6: Preparation time 15 minutes: Cooking time about 10 minutes: Croûtons freeze well

a secret from our kitchen

The easiest way to remove the seeds from a pomegranate is to halve them. Place a sieve over a bowl. Take each pomegranate half and hit the back of the skin side with the back of a spoon. The seeds will fall straight into the sieve. Apparently in Greece pomegranates are good luck – so if you are going to dinner with Greek friends, take one as a gift!

3 thick slices white bread
1 tablespoon olive oil
salt and pepper
1 romaine lettuce, roughly chopped
1 little gem lettuce, roughly chopped
3 good tablespoons roughly chopped fresh mint
100 g (4 oz) feta cheese, cut into 1cm (1/2 in) dice

50 g (2 oz) mixed pitted olives, halved
1 pomegranate, halved and with seeds removed (see Secret)

Dressing
6 tablespoons olive oil
3 tablespoons lemon juice
1 teaspoon caster sugar

Preheat the oven to 220°C/425°F/Gas 7.

Remove the crusts from the bread, cut into 2.5 cm (1 in) cubes, toss in the olive oil and spread in a large roasting tin in a single layer. Bake in the preheated oven for about 10 minutes or until golden brown and crisp. Set aside to cool, then season with salt and pepper.

Measure the ingredients for the dressing into a bowl and whisk until smooth.

Mix the lettuces, mint, feta and olives together in a large salad bowl. Toss the salad in the dressing just before serving. Sprinkle over the croûtons and pomegranate seeds.

To cook in the Aga Cook the croûtons in a large roasting tin on the lowest set of runners in the roasting oven for about 10 minutes, tossing occasionally. If your roasting oven is on the cool side, you may need to cook them directly on the floor.

Tip You can buy ready-made croûtons, but I don't think you can beat home-made ones. Make sure you add them after the salad has been dressed, otherwise they will go soggy.

ⓥ Oriental Noodle Salad

I have mixed oriental with country for this recipe, using British radishes instead of the traditional Japanese daikon or mooli. Carrots, spring onions and herbs are all often grown at home in the summer, so are perfect to use for a barbecue or picnic. This is a very different salad, much more interesting than the traditional rice or pasta salads you see on most buffet or picnic tables.

Serves 4–6 Preparation time 10 minutes: Cooking time about 5 minutes: Not suitable for freezing

100 g (4 oz) Blue Dragon medium rice noodles
1 carrot, peeled and coarsely grated
100 g (4 oz) beansprouts
4 spring onions, finely sliced on the diagonal
1 sheet nori seaweed, thinly sliced
6 red radishes, finely sliced
1 small red pepper, deseeded and finely sliced
5 tablespoons chopped fresh parsley or coriander (reserve the stalks)

Dressing
3 tablespoons sushi pickled ginger, finely chopped
175 ml (6 fl oz) rice wine vinegar or white wine vinegar
4 tablespoons soy sauce
6 tablespoons olive oil

a secret from our kitchen

This is a recipe I make at our demonstrations. I find people are never quite sure about seaweed, but once they see how easy it is to use, it always proves to be very popular. It is used in a sheet for sushi, but I have cut strands for this recipe. I find it easier to snip with scissors than cut with a knife.

Cook and soak the noodles according to the instructions on the packet, drain and refresh in cold water. Dry well.

Carefully mix the dry noodles with all the prepared vegetables.

Measure the dressing ingredients into a jug and whisk together. Pour half of the dressing over the noodle salad and toss gently to coat the salad. Cover and leave to marinate for a minimum of an hour.

To serve, dress with the remaining dressing.

Tip Nori seaweed can be bought in all good supermarkets in the Oriental section – it comes flat in a packet. I have used rice noodles here, as they are white when cooked, so look very attractive with the different colours of the vegetables. Use medium noodles, and not the very fine, as the latter can become a bit sticky. You can use egg noodles if preferred.

Fresh Salmon and Potato Salad with Herb Dressing

This recipe is perfect for picnics with friends, or for eating outdoors in the garden. All you need to go with it is some green salad and a loaf of crusty bread.

Serves 4–6 Preparation time 30 minutes: Cooking time 10–15 minutes: Not suitable for freezing

450 g (1 lb) salmon fillet
salt and pepper
450 g (1 lb) baby new potatoes
3 shallots, quartered
Dressing
2 tablespoons grainy mustard
2 tablespoons white wine vinegar

3 tablespoons olive oil
2 tablespoons capers
1 x 200 ml carton half-fat crème fraîche
4 tablespoons low-fat mayonnaise
3 tablespoons chopped fresh parsley
3 tablespoons snipped fresh chives

Preheat the oven to 160°C/325°F/Gas 3.

Season the salmon fillet, wrap in foil, place on a baking sheet and bake in the preheated oven for about 10–15 minutes until just done. Set aside to cool, then flake with a fork into large chunks.

Meanwhile, boil the potatoes and shallots together in boiling salted water for 10–15 minutes until the potatoes are tender. Drain. Cut each potato into quarters.

Put all the ingredients for the dressing into a bowl and whisk until blended. Pour over the hot, drained potatoes and shallots.

Carefully stir in the salmon chunks, season with salt and pepper, and leave to cool completely. Chill for about 20 minutes before serving.

To cook in the Aga Boil the potatoes in boiling water on the boiling plate for about 10 minutes until just done. Wrap the salmon in foil, sit on a baking sheet and slide on to the lowest set of runners in the roasting oven for about 10 minutes. Alternatively, you can cook the foil parcel in the simmering oven for about 15–20 minutes until just done.

Tip I have used shallots, but you could use a small onion instead. Pouring the dressing over the potatoes while warm helps the dressing to soak in and gives a lovely flavour. Do be careful when mixing the salad not to break up the salmon – it should stay in large chunks. If you are short of time, instead of poaching your own salmon, buy pre-packed hot-smoked salmon. Cooked by the hot-smoking method, it has a lovely intense flavour.

Thyme-marinated Prawns with a Squeeze of Lemon and Lime

I have used prawns only for these kebabs, as I think they look stunning. Keep the wedges of lemon and lime fairly chunky so that they retain their juice – you can then squeeze them over the prawns when eating. We had great fun deciding how to arrange the skewers for the photo. I managed with great persuasion to have them arranged in a jug, which everyone thought was a little unusual, but I think is much more fun than serving them piled on a plate.

Serves 4–6 (10 kebabs) Preparation time up to an hour including marinating:
Cooking time 10–15 minutes: Not suitable for freezing

1 head fennel
salt and pepper
2 tablespoons fresh thyme leaves
2 cloves garlic, crushed
3 tablespoons olive oil
1 red pepper, deseeded and cut into 20 wedges

2 large lemons, cut into 10 wedges
2 large limes, cut into 10 wedges
450 g (1 lb) raw tiger prawns (50), without heads or shells

You will need 10 long metal or wooden skewers

Cut the fennel in half lengthways and cut a triangle shape to remove the core. Peel the layers from the fennel and cut into 20 squares. Blanch the fennel in boiling salted water for about 4 minutes, drain and refresh in cold water until stone cold. Dry well.

Mix the thyme leaves, garlic and olive oil together in a bowl. Add the fennel, pepper, lemon and lime wedges and the prawns to the marinade, season with salt and pepper, and stir so everything is coated. Cover in clingfilm and chill for no longer than an hour.

Thread two prawns, then a lemon wedge, a pepper wedge, a square of fennel, one prawn, a lime wedge, a pepper wedge, a square of fennel and two prawns on to each skewer. Repeat using all ten skewers.

To charcoal-grill, cook the kebabs on a hot barbecue for about 4 minutes on each side until the prawns have turned pink. Or, to conventionally grill, place the kebabs on a baking sheet and slide under a preheated grill for about 4 minutes on each side until the prawns are pink.

Serve hot, squeezing the lemon and lime wedges over the prawns.

continued next page

To cook in the Aga Arrange the kebabs on a baking sheet and slide on to the top set of runners in the roasting oven for about 4 minutes on each side or until the prawns turn pink.

Tip For an extra special occasion, buy king prawns or large North Atlantic prawns with shell and heads on – they are very messy to eat, but look fantastic and taste delicious. They are more expensive than tiger prawns, but worth it. Always use fresh thyme. It is a wonderful herb, and there are many different varieties. Common thyme is the one sold in most supermarkets, but lemon thyme and golden thyme are very easy to grow at home too. Cut back after flowering, just above the old wood, and they will continue year after year.

Twisted Chicken and Courgette Spicy Kebabs

This is a fun recipe to make that's delicious to eat. It's best eaten immediately it's cooked. Keep the skin on the courgettes, as it stops them from falling apart and makes them look much prettier (see picture on page 133).

Serves 4–6 Preparation time 10 minutes: Cooking time 15 minutes: Not suitable for freezing

4 chicken breasts, boneless and skinless

2 large courgettes

Marinade

1 x 150 g tub natural yoghurt

1 clove garlic, crushed

1 tablespoon garam masala

1 teaspoon paprika

$^1/_2$ teaspoon ground ginger

1 tablespoon tomato purée

1 tablespoon lemon juice

1 tablespoon sunflower oil

You will need 16 metal or wooden skewers

Measure all the ingredients for the marinade into a large bowl and mix together. Slice the chicken breasts into four strips lengthways. Toss the chicken in the marinade, cover and leave for as long as possible, or overnight if time allows.

Preheat the oven to 200°C/ 400°F/Gas 6, or the chicken can be cooked on the barbecue.

Using a wide potato peeler, slice 16 ribbons lengthways from the courgettes. Lay a ribbon of courgette on top of a strip of chicken and thread (weaving) on to a skewer.

Cook on a baking sheet in the preheated oven for about 15 minutes until golden brown and cooked through. Alternatively, cook on the barbecue, for about 5–10 minutes on each side.

Serve at once, with a freshly dressed green salad, or the Oriental Noodle Salad on page 130.

To cook in the Aga Slide the baking sheet on to the top set of runners in the roasting oven for about 10–15 minutes or until golden brown and cooked through.

Tip If using wooden skewers for kebabs on a barbecue, soak them in water first to prevent them burning.

a secret from our kitchen

Unless you have a very well maintained and slug-free vegetable garden, I would recommend growing courgettes in pots – I find it much easier. Grease the outside of the pots with Vaseline and the slugs will slide off and not be able to reach the courgette plant (this doesn't hurt the slug, they just think they are on a waterslide!). Keep the pots by the back door so you can keep an eye on growth and catch the courgettes before they turn into marrows. The courgette flower is pretty as a garnish too.

Fresh Mango Chicken with Watercress Salad

This is just perfect for a picnic or a cold lunch, or for a buffet. It's a little similar to the classic Coronation chicken, but much fresher and more up to date.

Serves 6 Preparation time 15 minutes: Not suitable for freezing

1 large ripe mango
750 g (1³/4 lb) cooked chicken breasts, skinless and boneless (see Secret)
1 x 85 g bag fresh watercress
6 long chives

Sauce
1 x 200 g tub low-fat Greek yoghurt
4 tablespoons low-calorie mayonnaise
2 tablespoons lemon juice
3 tablespoons mango chutney
1 tablespoon curry powder
1 tablespoon paprika
salt and pepper

For the sauce, put the yoghurt, mayonnaise, lemon juice, mango chutney and spices in a large bowl and mix together until smooth. Season with salt and pepper.

Cut the flesh from the mango either side of the flat mango stone in the middle (see page 30). Remove the peel using a knife. Slice the flesh into thin slices. Cut four slices into small dice and mix these with the sauce in the bowl.

Cut the cooked chicken into long strips, and mix in with the sauce.

Arrange the watercress and mango slices around the edges of a flat platter. Spoon the chicken and sauce into the centre of the platter and arrange the whole chives in a criss-cross pattern across the top.

Tip You can, of course, use full-fat Greek yoghurt and mayonnaise if preferred, but most of us like to cut the calorie count wherever possible.

a secret from our kitchen

You can make this recipe with freshly cooked turkey too. I always think it is nicer to poach chicken breasts rather than buy them ready-cooked. Sit the chicken breasts in a saucepan, just cover with water, then add some seasonings and flavourings, and simmer over a low heat until just cooked, about 15 minutes. The chicken is then very succulent and not dry at all.

Sticky Spare Ribs

These spare ribs, glazed in a sticky rich sauce, are perfect for a barbecue.
Summer and barbecues always make me smile and remember many happy times
– outdoors in the garden, warmth, relaxing with friends, delicious food. I don't
have a barbecue at home, but I do have a Chiminea (an outdoor pottery fire).
I just put a grill rack into the open hole and cook on the top. It takes longer than
a barbecue, but it's very rustic, and it feels like I am cooking with nature!

Serves 2 (4 each) Preparation time 10 minutes: Cooking time 50 minutes:
Freezes well raw in the marinade

8 single spare ribs

Marinade

2 tablespoons runny honey

1 tablespoon soy sauce

1 tablespoon Worcestershire sauce

1 tablespoon tomato purée

1 teaspoon Chinese five-spice powder

1 small clove garlic, crushed

Preheat the oven to 200°C/400°F/Gas 6, or light the barbecue.

Mix all the marinade ingredients together in a large bowl. Add the spare ribs
and coat in the mixture. Cover the bowl with clingfilm and leave to marinate for
at least an hour, or overnight if time allows.

Tip the spare ribs into a roasting tin and roast in the preheated oven for about
45–50 minutes, turning over halfway, until cooked through, shiny and crisp.
Alternatively, cook on the barbecue for about 30–40 minutes.

To cook in the Aga Slide the roasting tin on to the floor of the roasting oven for
about 40 minutes, turning halfway, until crisp and shiny and cooked through.

Tip If you are unable to find Chinese five-spice powder, you can use a pinch each
of paprika, cayenne, allspice and nutmeg. Take care when cooking spare ribs on
the barbecue. Make sure the coals have died down to a glow, or a gas one is on
low, otherwise the ribs will brown too much before they are cooked through.

Quick Herby Pepperoni Scone Pizza with Double Cheese

Everyone loves pizza, so try this one, made with a scone base instead of a dough base. A pizza is perfect for eating outdoors, or for taking on a picnic. I remember as a child sitting on the grass bank of the river at Hurley where we lived, munching away, watching the boats go by. Lovely memories . . .

Serves 6 Preparation time 15 minutes: Cooking time 20 minutes: Not suitable for freezing

Quick scone base
175 g (6 oz) self-raising flour
1 teaspoon baking powder
65 g (1¹/₂ oz) butter, cut into small pieces
50 g (2 oz) Cheddar cheese, grated
2 tablespoons chopped fresh thyme
salt and pepper
1 small egg
about 75 ml (2¹/₂ fl oz) milk

Topping
3 tablespoons tomato purée
2 cloves garlic, crushed
1 green pepper, deseeded and thinly
  sliced
4 spring onions, thinly sliced
50 g (2 oz) Cheddar cheese, grated
50 g (2 oz) pepperoni, thinly sliced
150 g (5 oz) mozzarella cheese, grated
50 g (2 oz) black olives, stoned

a secret from our kitchen

This scone base is ideal for small savoury scones too. Just make the scone base as above and roll to a thickness of about 5 cm (2 in). Cut out rounds with a 5 cm (2 in) floured scone cutter, then bake for about 12 minutes at the same temperature as here. The scones are perfect with something like the Red Pepper and Tomato Soup on page 16.

Preheat the oven to 200°C/400°F/Gas 6.

First make the scone base. Measure the flour, baking powder and butter into a bowl. Rub in the butter using your fingertips until the mixture resembles fine breadcrumbs. Stir in the cheese, thyme and some salt and pepper. In a small measuring jug beat the egg, then pour in the milk until it measures 100 ml (3 fl oz). Pour the egg mixture into the flour and mix together until a soft dough is formed (this can also be made in a mixer using a dough hook). Tip the dough on to a floured work surface. Roll out using a rolling pin to a 33 cm (13 in) circle (it should be fairly thin). Slide the base on to a large greased baking sheet.

Spread the tomato purée over the base right to the edge. Sprinkle over the garlic, pepper, spring onion and Cheddar cheese. Top with pepperoni, mozzarella and olives, and season with salt and pepper.

Slide the baking sheet into the preheated oven and bake for about 15–20 minutes or until the pizza is golden brown on top and cooked underneath.

To cook in the Aga Slide the baking sheet on to the floor of the roasting oven for about 15–20 minutes until the pizza is golden brown on top and crisp underneath.

puddings

Classic Rice Pudding with Flapjack Topping

I think classic recipes like rice pudding have been forgotten a little, but really there is nothing nicer. As I always stir some golden syrup into my rice pudding for sweetness, I have taken the idea a little further, and have mixed the syrup with oats to make a different topping.

Serves 4 Preparation time 5 minutes: Cooking time 2– 2½ hours: Not suitable for freezing

butter

50 g (2 oz) pudding rice

25 g (1 oz) caster sugar

600 ml (1 pint) full-fat milk

Topping

25 g (1 oz) porridge oats

100 g (4 oz) golden syrup

Preheat the oven to 160°C/325°F/Gas 3. You will need a buttered 1 litre (1¾ pint) shallow ovenproof dish.

Wash the rice under running cold water and dry well. Sprinkle over the base of the buttered dish. Sprinkle over the sugar, pour in the milk and dot knobs of butter – about 15g (½ oz) – into the milk.

Bake in the preheated oven for about 2 hours until just golden brown and thick (the rice absorbs most of the milk). Remove from the oven and turn on the grill while making the topping.

Mix together the oats and syrup to make a thick gooey mixture. Dollop over the top of the set rice pudding as evenly as possible (don't worry if there are gaps). Pop under the grill for about 5 minutes until bubbling (the syrup and oats will spread a little while under the grill).

Set aside for a few minutes for the topping to crisp up a little, and serve warm.

To cook in the Aga Slide the pudding on to the lowest set of runners in the roasting oven for about 25 minutes until golden brown. Transfer to the simmering oven for a further 2 hours until the rice is cooked and the pudding is nearly set (but still a tiny bit runny). Dollop the topping over the pudding and slide on to the second set of runners in the roasting oven for about 10 minutes until golden brown and crisp.

Tip It looks as though there is a tiny amount of rice here, but it absorbs the milk and gives a perfect pudding. Use a shallow wide-surfaced pudding dish; the topping would be too thick in a deep, narrow dish.

a secret from our kitchen

If you only have semi-skimmed milk in the fridge, use this for the pudding, but enrich it with a couple of tablespoons of double cream.

Rhubarb Crumble with a Hint of Whisky

Whoever invented the crumble is a genius. (I reckon it was my mother, as I think she makes the best!) I do like a lot of topping though, so this has a lot: half of it goes soggy from the fruit liquid, and the top stays crisp. Of course you can use other fruits if you do not wish to use rhubarb.

Serves 4–6 Preparation 10 minutes: Cooking time 40 minutes: Freezes well

900 g (2 lb) rhubarb, chopped
    into 2.5 cm (1 in) pieces
3 tablespoons whisky
100 g (4 oz) muscovado sugar

Crumble topping
175 g (6 oz) plain flour
75 g (3 oz) cold butter, chopped into
    small pieces
75 g (3 oz) caster sugar

Preheat the oven to 180°C/350°F/Gas 4. You will need a shallow 1 litre (1³/₄ pint) ovenproof dish.

To make the topping, sieve the flour into a bowl. Rub the butter into the flour using your hands until the mixture resembles fine breadcrumbs. Stir in the caster sugar. (You can do this in a processor to save time, if preferred.) Arrange the rhubarb and whisky in the base of the ovenproof dish, sprinkle over the sugar, and spoon over the crumble. Slide into the preheated oven and cook for about 30– 40 minutes or until golden brown on top and bubbling round the edges.

Serve with pouring cream.

To cook in the Aga Slide the ovenproof dish on to the grid shelf on the floor in the roasting oven with the cold sheet on the second set of runners, and cook for about 30 minutes until golden brown. Transfer the hot cold sheet to the simmering oven and cook for a further 20 minutes until piping hot and bubbling.

Tip The joy of a crumble is that you do not need to cook the prepared fruit ahead. Whether it is apple, plum or blackcurrant, all the fruit can go in raw. Some recipes do advise you to cook the fruit ahead, but there is really no need.

a secret from our kitchen

Take early pickings from your rhubarb plants, as they are sweeter and less tough. Rhubarb should be pulled from the ground, and not cut. In France they always peel rhubarb, but we think the pink skin is the best part, and so pretty.

Naughty Plum and Almond Puff

In my opinion, the best fruits to grow in the garden are Victoria plums. They are very traditional and the trees give high yields. You only need one tree to benefit from a whole crop of fruit. Light pruning in spring will ensure that the branches do not become over-laden with fruit and snap. I remember visiting my grandmother in Wiltshire as a child and collecting fallen plums from the ground.

Serves 6 Preparation time 10 minutes: Cooking time 25– 30 minutes: Not suitable for freezing

a secret from our kitchen

Mary and I devised a recipe for her latest book using brioche and apricots. Everyone loved it, and I wanted another recipe just as easy and delicious. See what you think! You can replace the plums with apricots or pears, depending on what is in season.

1 x 375 g packet fresh ready-rolled puff pastry

100 g (4 oz) golden marzipan

8 large fresh plums, halved and stoned

a sprinkling of ground cinnamon

1 x 250 g tub mascarpone cheese

1– 2 tablespoons demerara sugar

1 egg, beaten with a little milk, to glaze

Preheat the oven to 200°C/400°F/Gas 6, and preheat a baking sheet in the oven to get very hot.

Unroll the pastry from the packet and roll out a little more to give a 30 x 25 cm (12 x 10 in) rectangle. Arrange on bakewell paper or non-stick graphite paper. Using a sharp knife, score a border in the pastry 1 cm (1/2 in) from the edge – do not cut right the way through, just halfway. Prick all over the centre with a fork (but not the border).

Coarsely grate the marzipan and sprinkle evenly over the pastry base within the scored lines. Arrange the halved plums (cut side up) on top of the marzipan, within the lines. Sprinkle each plum with a little cinnamon.

Spoon a teaspoon of mascarpone into the hollow centre of each plum and sprinkle the plums with a little demerara sugar. Glaze the border of the pastry with the beaten egg and milk.

Remove the very hot baking sheet from the oven, and slide it under the paper and tart. Return to the oven and and bake for about 25–30 minutes until the pastry is cooked and golden brown (check it is cooked underneath) and the plums are tender.

Serve hot with a dollop of the remaining mascarpone on the side.

To cook in the Aga Slide the tart on a cold baking sheet on to the grid shelf on the floor of the roasting oven for about 10 minutes. Remove the grid shelf and slide the baking sheet directly on to the floor of the roasting oven for a further 10 minutes until the pastry is golden brown (check underneath too) and the plums are tender. If your Aga is a little slow, you may need to cook on the floor of the roasting oven for the whole time.

Sunday Lunch Apple and Pear Tart

There is nothing nicer than a Sunday lunch at home with family and friends. I remember many such very fondly: delicious food, then, after lunch, a walk through the woods with the dogs, back home, fire lit and feet up! This tart is very large, but worth doing, as you can then enjoy it for the rest of the week (or freeze the remainder).

Serves 8–10 Preparation time 15 minutes plus resting time for the pastry: Cooking time about 50 minutes: Freezes well

a **secret** from our **kitchen**

As you can imagine, we have a very busy kitchen, so often need to do things ahead. This tart can be made in advance and reheats very well: do so either in a low oven or in the simmering oven of the Aga. Do be sure to serve it when it is warm and not hot straight from the oven, as a custard filling needs to 'set' for about 10 minutes once removed from the oven.

4 dessert apples, peeled, quartered and thinly sliced
4 small barely ripe pears, peeled, quartered and thinly sliced
2 tablespoons apricot jam
2 tablespoons water
Pastry
225 g (8 oz) plain flour
100 g (4 oz) butter, cubed

25 g (1 oz) caster sugar
1 egg yolk
2 tablespoons cold water
Custard
5 eggs
1 teaspoon vanilla extract
175 g (6 oz) caster sugar
300 ml (10 fl oz) double cream

Preheat the oven to 200°C/400°F/Gas 6, and preheat a flat baking sheet to get very hot.

To make the pastry, measure the flour, butter and sugar into a processor and whizz until the mixture resembles breadcrumbs. Add the egg yolk and water and whizz again until a dough is formed (you can also make this by hand). Wrap in clingfilm and transfer to the fridge to rest for about 30 minutes or however long time allows.

Roll the pastry out on a floured surface to fit a 28 cm (11 in) loose-bottomed flan tin, ensuring there are no holes. Arrange the sliced apples and pears over the base of the pastry.

For the custard, whisk the eggs and vanilla together in a bowl. Add the sugar and cream and whisk again until smooth. Pour into the flan case.

Very carefully (so as not to make a crack in the pastry), transfer the flan tin on to the very hot baking sheet in the oven and bake for about 25 minutes. Lower the temperature to 180°C/350°F/Gas 4, and bake for a further 25 minutes until the custard is set and the pastry is crisp.

Remove the baking sheet from the oven and leave the tart to cool for about 10 minutes before cutting.

While cooling, melt the jam and water together in a pan and boil until it becomes a glaze (you may need to whisk it a little). Using a pastry brush, brush the glaze over the top of the tart.

Serve warm with crème fraîche.

To cook in the Aga Slide the tin directly on to the floor of the roasting oven for about 20 minutes. Slide the grid shelf on to the floor of the roasting oven with the tart on top and the cold sheet on the second set of runners (to prevent the top from becoming too brown) for a further 25 minutes until the pastry is crisp and the custard just set.

Tip If you don't want to make the pastry yourself, you can buy ready-made tart cases, which are very good. To make the finished tart look particularly professional, arrange the apples and pears alternating in a circle. Do not forget the glaze, as it makes all the difference.

Frangipane Pudding with Autumn Fruits

Blackberries (brambles) grow freely in the hedgerows everywhere. They can be very intrusive so we don't grow them at work, but the garden is surrounded by them. Picking berries on a long walk reminds me so much of my childhood. This pudding is a little like eve's pudding, but with a frangipane topping and autumn fruits instead of apple.

a secret from our kitchen

At work, we have fruit cages where we grow redcurrants, blackcurrants, raspberries and gooseberries. They are well netted under the cages, too, due to the birds' love of them – the nets and cages do the trick. We just freeze them as they are in plastic boxes. The easiest way to take redcurrants off their stems is to put the stem between the prongs of a fork and push downwards – they will fly off!

Serves 6 Preparation time 10 minutes: Cooking time 35–40 minutes: Not suitable for freezing

butter for greasing
225 g (8 oz) blackberries
6 ripe plums, stoned and thinly sliced
2 dessert apples, peeled, cored and cut into small chunks
1 tablespoon caster sugar

Frangipane
175 g (6 oz) butter, softened
175 g (6 oz) caster sugar
3 eggs, beaten
175 g (6 oz) ground almonds
25 g (1 oz) plain flour
1 teaspoon almond extract

Preheat the oven to 180°C/350°F/Gas 4. Butter a 1.5 litre (2³/₄ pint) ovenproof dish. Arrange the fruits evenly over the base of the buttered dish, then sprinkle over the sugar.

To make the frangipane, measure the butter and sugar into a processor and whizz until creamy. Add the eggs and whizz again (do not worry if it looks a little curdled at this stage). Add the ground almonds, flour and almond extract and whizz again until all the ingredients are combined.

Spoon over the top of the fruits (don't worry about being too neat). Transfer to the oven and bake for about 35 minutes until firm to the touch and golden brown. If the top begins to get too brown during the cooking, cover with foil.

Serve warm, with custard, cream, vanilla ice cream or crème fraîche.

To cook in the Aga Slide the dish on to the lowest set of runners in the roasting oven for about 35–40 minutes until golden brown and firm to the touch. If the top begins to get too brown during cooking, slide the cold sheet in on the second set of runners.

Tip I always use extracts rather than essences, as they have a much stronger, more natural flavour. With vanilla and almond extracts this is especially important. We did a blind tasting for a magazine of all the different vanilla flavourings, and found the extract to be the best – even better than a vanilla pod.

Honey-glazed Pineapple with Rum and Ginger

This lovely recipe is low in fat – but only if you don't follow my suggestion of serving it with crème fraîche! You can use Malibu or brandy if you prefer them to rum.

Serves 4 Preparation time 10 minutes: Cooking time 15 minutes: Not suitable for freezing

1 medium, just ripe, fresh pineapple
3 tablespoons dark rum
3 tablespoons runny honey
3 tablespoons syrup from the ginger jar

4 tablespoons water
3 bulbs stem ginger from a jar, finely
   chopped

Remove the top from the pineapple. Peel and cut in four lengthways. Cut out the core and slice each quarter lengthways into four long wedges (giving you 16 strips).

Place the pineapple wedges into a wide-based saucepan (so they are in a single layer). Pour over the other ingredients, except the stem ginger, cover and bring to the boil. Lower the heat and simmer (do not allow to boil) for about 15 minutes until just tender – the pineapple should still hold its shape and be just tender to eat.

Using a slotted spoon, transfer the pineapple to a serving dish and sprinkle over the stem ginger. Reduce the sauce to about 4 tablespoons, or to a thin coating consistency, and pour over the pineapple.

Serve four wedges per person (making sure every plate has stem ginger too). Pour a little sauce over the top, and add a dollop of crème fraîche if you like.

To cook in the Aga Bring the pan to simmering point on the simmering plate, cover and transfer to the simmering oven for about 15 minutes until just tender.

Tip I have served this warm and cold, and both are equally delicious. If serving cold, it can be made up to 24 hours ahead. Stem ginger is wonderful and great in so many recipes, but do not confuse it with fresh or crystallised ginger. If a pineapple is ripe, it will smell sweet. If you can pull a leaf out easily from the top, this is a sign of ripeness too.

Pumpkin and Cinnamon Baked Cheesecake

Around Hallowe'en, when I was writing this book, so many of my friends asked me for a sweet pumpkin recipe (they had overdosed on pumpkin soup), that I had to invent one, so here it is.

Serves 6–8 Preparation time 20 minutes (50 if using fresh pumpkin): Cooking time 1½ hours: Not suitable for freezing

a secret from our kitchen

Using fresh pumpkin gives a slightly stronger flavour, but cooking it is time-consuming, so an alternative is to use the microwave. Sprinkle 4 tablespoons water over the pumpkin chunks in a bowl, cover with clingfilm and cook on a medium heat (600 W) for about 5–6 minutes until tender. Leave to stand for 2 minutes, then whizz as here.

butter for greasing
400 g (14 oz) fresh pumpkin
   (or 1 x 400 g can pumpkin purée)
900 g (2 lb) full-fat cream cheese
300 g (10 oz) caster sugar
25 g (1 oz) plain flour, sieved
2 teaspoons ground cinnamon

5 eggs, beaten
2 tablespoons dark rum or brandy
150ml (5 fl oz) double cream, lightly
   whipped
Base
100 g (4 oz) Hobnob biscuits, crushed
50 g (2 oz) butter, melted

Preheat the oven to 160°C/325°F/Gas 3. Grease the sides of a 23 cm (9 in) springform or loose-bottomed tin.

To make the base, mix the ingredients together and press into the base of the tin with the back of a spoon until even. Transfer to the fridge to firm.

To make the filling, cut the fresh pumpkin into even-sized small pieces and boil for about 30 minutes until tender (this will depend on the size of the pumpkin pieces). Drain and whizz in a processor until smooth.

Measure the cream cheese into a large mixing bowl with the sugar, flour and cinnamon, and whisk with an electric hand whisk until fluffy. Continuing to whisk, gradually add the beaten eggs until smooth, then stir in the rum or brandy. Stir in the pumpkin purée and mix until smooth.

Pour the mixture over the chilled base and bake in the preheated oven for about 1½ hours or until the filling has set (if it begins to get too brown, cover with foil). Remove from the oven, release the edges with a palette knife, and set aside to cool. Once cool, remove from the tin, transfer to a serving dish, and chill.

Spread the whipped cream over the top, and dust with a little more cinnamon to serve.

To cook in the Aga Bake the cheesecake on the grid shelf on the floor of the roasting oven for about 40– 45 minutes, with the cold sheet on the second set of runners, until set on top but with a wobble in the middle (if it begins to get too brown on top you may need to change the cold sheet halfway through). Transfer the hot cold sheet to the centre of the simmering oven, sit the cheesecake on top, and bake for a further hour until set.

Tip The cheesecake puffs up when it comes out of the oven, but once it cools will dip and crack slightly – don't worry, this is part of its charm! Releasing the edges with a palette knife just before it cools will prevent it from cracking too much.

Silky Passion Cheesecake

I seem to have spent forever getting this recipe right, but I am finally there! To get the most flavour from passionfruit, you usually add all the pips, but I wanted to have a pip-free dessert, yet still with the intense flavour. If you don't want to sieve the passionfruit, you can put all the pips in, but then, obviously, there is no need to infuse them in the cream. It can be made up to 2 hours ahead.

Serves 6 Preparation time 15 minutes: Chilling time 4 hours minimum: Not suitable for freezing

400 g (14 oz) full-fat fromage frais
150 g (5 oz) caster sugar
8 small passionfruit
150 ml (5 fl oz) single cream
1 x 11 g packet (about 5 teaspoons)
    powdered gelatine
300 ml (10 fl oz) double cream, lightly
    whipped

sprigs of fresh mint or lavender, to garnish
icing sugar, to dust
Biscuit base
175 g (6 oz) digestive biscuits
75 g (3 oz) butter, melted
25 g (1 oz) demerara sugar

a secret from our kitchen

This is an easy way of dissolving powdered gelatine, so long as your cream is hot. If when mixing in the gelatine, you find it is still a little grainy, carefully heat the cream bowl over boiling water, whisking all the time, until the gelatine has just dissolved (do not allow the cream to boil).

Use either ten 7 cm (2¾ in) cooking rings or a 20 cm (8 in) deep loose-bottomed cake tin or springform tin. If using cooking rings, arrange on a baking sheet.

For the base, put the biscuits into a plastic bag and crush with a rolling pin until they are fine crumbs. Tip into a bowl and mix with the butter and sugar. Press evenly over the base of the cake tin or rings. Transfer to the fridge to firm up.

To make the cheesecake, measure the fromage frais and sugar into a large bowl. Scoop out the seeds from the passionfruit and sieve over a measuring jug to give 100 ml (3½ fl oz) of juice. Mix the juice in with the fromage frais.

Tip the passionfruit seeds into a saucepan with the single cream, and carefully bring to the boil. Once the cream is piping hot, strain into a bowl and immediately sprinkle in the gelatine. Whisk until the gelatine has dissolved, then immediately pour into the fromage frais bowl. Pour this mixture into the whipped cream and carefully mix until smooth with no lumps.

Pour into the cake tin or rings on top of the firm biscuit base. Chill in the fridge for a minimum of 4 hours.

Using a small palette knife, go round the edges of the rings to release them, and serve the little cheesecakes on small plates garnished with mint or lavender and a dusting of icing sugar. Likewise, with the large cake tin, release from the tin and garnish, then serve in wedges.

Tip If your passionfruit are a little dry inside and you don't have enough juice for 100 ml (3½ fl oz), then top up with a little orange juice.

Bursting Blueberry Soured Cream Dessert Cake

This recipe was kindly given to me by my lovely Canadian friend Cheryl, who lives nearby in Penn. I first had it when I went to her cottage for dinner, and just adored it. I hope you do too.

Serves 8 Preparation time 10 minutes: Cooking time about an hour: Not suitable for freezing

Base
225 g (8 oz) self-raising flour

100 g (4 oz) butter, softened

100 g (4 oz) caster sugar

1^1/$_2$ teaspoons baking powder

1 egg

Filling
600 ml (1 pint) soured cream

175 g (6 oz) caster sugar

2 egg yolks

1 teaspoon vanilla extract

350 g (12 oz) fresh blueberries

Preheat the oven to 180°C/350°F/Gas 4. You will need a 23 cm (9 in) springform tin.

First make the base. Measure the flour, butter, sugar, baking powder and egg into a processor and whizz until it forms a soft dough (you can also do this by hand in a bowl). Tip on to a lightly floured work surface and roll out to the size of the tin. Transfer the dough into the base of the tin. If it breaks, don't worry, you can push it in with your fingers (it doesn't need to be neat).

Measure the soured cream, sugar, egg yolks and vanilla into a bowl and beat until all is mixed together.

Sprinkle the blueberries on to the base and pour the filling over the top. Transfer to the preheated oven, and bake for about an hour or until the edges are lightly browned and the mixture is just set in the middle. Leave to cool in the tin.

Once cold, transfer to a serving dish. Serve cold with extra blueberries if liked, dusted with a little icing sugar.

To cook in the Aga Slide the tin on to the grid shelf on the floor of the roasting oven with the cold sheet on the second set of runners for about 40 minutes until lightly golden brown round the edges but still with a wobble in the middle. Transfer the hot cold sheet to the centre of the simmering oven, put the cake tin on top and bake for a further 30 minutes until just set in the middle.

Tip This dessert is rustic, crinkly round the top, with purple edges where the blueberries burst. Use raspberries instead of blueberries if you prefer.

Glazed Ginger, Orange and Ricotta Cake

This can be served as a dessert or at tea-time. It's a continental cake, something you might enjoy with a latte in a back-street café in a village on the Amalfi coast.

Serves 8 Preparation time 10 minutes: Cooking time 40 minutes: Freezes well

150 g (5 oz) butter, softened, plus extra for greasing
1 x 250 g tub ricotta cheese
6 eggs, separated
150 g (5 oz) ground almonds
150 g (5 oz) caster sugar
finely grated zest of 2 oranges

4 bulbs stem ginger, chopped into tiny pieces (the size of raisins)
icing sugar, to dust
Icing
2 tablespoons thin-cut marmalade
1 tablespoon ginger syrup from the jar

Preheat the oven to 180°C/350°F/Gas 4. Grease a 23 cm (9 in) springform tin and base-line with non-stick paper.

Mix the butter, ricotta, egg yolks, almonds, sugar, orange zest and chopped ginger together in a large bowl. Beat with a wooden spoon until smooth.

Whisk the egg whites in a separate bowl with an electric hand whisk until soft peaks. Carefully fold the whites into the ricotta mixture.

Pour into the lined cake tin and bake in the preheated oven for 30–35 minutes until risen and golden brown on top. Leave to cool a little in the tin. Carefully remove from the tin, peel off the paper and transfer to a serving plate.

To make the icing, melt the marmalade and ginger syrup in a small pan and pour over the warm cake. Serve warm or cold, dusted with a little icing sugar.

To cook in the Aga Slide the cake tin on to the grid shelf on the floor of the roasting oven with the cold sheet on the second set of runners for about 20 minutes or until golden brown and set around the edges. Transfer the hot cold sheet to the centre of the simmering oven and put the cake on top. Continue to bake for a further 20 minutes or until just set in the middle.

Tip The cake has a slightly grainy texture (because of the ricotta), but is lovely and light to eat. It will keep for up to three days in the fridge very happily.

Continental Chocolate Dessert Cake with Bailey's

This is a rich chocolate cake, which uses ground almonds instead of flour. It's perfect for a special occasion, as it's more of a dessert cake than a tea-time cake.

Serves 6–8 Preparation time 15 minutes: Cooking time 15– 20 minutes: Freezes well, unfilled.

butter for greasing
265 g (9½ oz) plain Bournville chocolate
6 eggs, 5 of them separated
215 g (7½ oz) caster sugar
150 g (5 oz) ground almonds

Filling
300 ml (10 fl oz) double cream, whipped
2 tablespoons Bailey's Irish Cream
450 g (1 lb) soft mixed fruits, eg raspberries, blueberries and strawberries
icing sugar, to dust

Preheat the oven to 180°C/350°F/Gas 4. Grease and base-line two 20cm (8 in) round sandwich cake tins.

Break the chocolate into a bowl and melt over a saucepan of hot water until just melted (do not allow to become too hot). Stir the chocolate until smooth.

Whisk the 5 egg whites until stiff but not dry. Place the 5 egg yolks and the whole egg in a separate large bowl with the sugar, and whisk together until thick and light in colour. Whisk the ground almonds, melted chocolate and 1 tablespoon of egg whites into the yolk mixture.

Carefully fold in the remaining egg whites, and turn into the prepared tins. Gently slide into the preheated oven and bake for about 15 minutes, turning round halfway through, until firm on top but just soft in the middle (the cakes will have a pale crust on top).

Allow the cakes to cool in their tins for about 10 minutes before turning out on to a wire rack. Cover with a clean tea-towel and leave to cool completely.

For the filling, mix together the whipped cream and Bailey's. Spread half the cream on one cake and scatter a third of the fruit over the top. Arrange the second cake on top, spread the remaining cream on top and scatter over the remaining fruit. Dust with icing sugar, garnish with fresh raspberry or strawberry leaves if liked, and serve.

To cook in the Aga Slide the cake tins on to the grid shelf on the floor of the roasting oven with the cold shelf on the second set of runners. Bake for about 15–20 minutes, turning halfway through, until firm on top but soft in the middle.

a secret from our kitchen

When using fruits for a filling, always use fresh fruit in season. You can buy frozen bags of mixed fruit, but they have a lot of juice when defrosted and can be mushy. They are great for making a quick coulis, though. Whizz a 225 g (8 oz) bag in a processor with 2 heaped tablespoons icing sugar and 1 tablespoon water until a purée. Sieve and serve as a coulis or sauce for dessert.

Wicked Chocolate and Nectarine Steamed Pudding

After devising this recipe, I chatted to friends, and I now realise that chocolate and nectarine is rather an unusual combination. In our family, however, it's well known – we love chocolate mousse with nectarines! I have also tested the recipe using two ripe Williams pears, cut into pieces, which is delicious too.

Serves 6–8 Preparation time 10 minutes: Cooking time 1½ hours: Not suitable for freezing

a secret from our kitchen

For a steamed pudding or Christmas pudding, it is important to make a pleat in the foil over the top of the pudding basin (as here). This allows the pudding to rise without bursting the foil. If you fold the edges of the foil in tightly against and around the basin, there is no need to tie it on with a piece of string (which is how it used to be done).

175 g (6 oz) butter, softened, plus extra for greasing
25 g (1 oz) cocoa powder
3 tablespoons boiling water
150 g (5 oz) self-raising flour
1 rounded teaspoon baking powder
175 g (6 oz) light muscovado sugar

3 eggs
2 ripe nectarines, peeled and cut into cubes (about the size of hazelnuts)

Sauce
100 g (4 oz) continental plain chocolate, broken into pieces
150 ml (5 fl oz) pouring double cream

You will need a 1.2 litre (2 pint) pudding basin. Cut a square of foil to fit in the base of the basin and butter it well.

Sieve the cocoa powder into a large mixing bowl. Add the boiling water, and whisk together to make a thick paste. Add the remaining pudding ingredients, except for the nectarines, and whisk together, using an electric hand whisk, until smooth. Stir in the nectarine pieces.

Pour the mixture into the buttered, foil-lined basin and level the top. Cut a double piece of foil about 23 cm (9 in) square, generously butter one side, and make a pleat across the middle. Cover the basin with the foil, buttered side down, and fold in the edges to seal the top tightly (so no steam can escape).

Transfer the basin to a large deep saucepan. Fill the saucepan with enough cold water to come halfway up the pudding basin. Bring to the boil, cover and simmer over a low heat for about 2 hours or until the pudding is firm and well risen. Don't let the water level drop too much.

Carefully remove the pudding from the saucepan, and leave to stand for about 5 minutes. Remove the foil, loosen the edges, and tip out on to a serving plate. Remove the foil square.

Whilst the pudding is cooking, make the sauce. Slowly melt together the chocolate and cream in a bowl over a pan of very hot water, stirring, until runny and smooth. Do not allow the bowl to touch the water, and make sure the

continued next page

chocolate and cream do not get too hot. Once the chocolate has melted, stir to mix evenly. Remove from the heat, but leave the bowl sitting over the pan to keep warm.

Pour the sauce over the steamed pudding to serve.

To cook in the Aga Make the pudding as above. Bring to the boil on the boiling plate, then cover and transfer to the simmering oven for about $1^{1}/_{2}$ hours or until the pudding is firm and cooked.

Tip If you prefer, you can make eight individual puddings (if you have eight small basins): bake these in an oven preheated to 180°C/350°F/Gas 4 for about $1^{1}/_{2}$ hours. The sauce is wicked and delicious but you can serve with extra cream too!

Quick Chocolate and Chestnut Mousse

I prefer a lighter mousse to a rich indulgent one. This really is so quick and easy: there's no gelatine or eggs – just deliciousness! I always use Bournville chocolate, which is perfect for melting.

Serves 6– 8 Preparation time 10 minutes: Not suitable for freezing

225 g (8 oz) Bournville chocolate, broken into pieces

1 x 435g can unsweetened chestnut purée

1 x 200ml tub full-fat crème fraîche

100 g (4 oz) icing sugar, sieved

300 ml (10 fl oz) double cream, lightly whipped

To serve

100 g (4 oz) fresh raspberries

pouring cream

a secret from our kitchen

If you do not wish to buy metal rings, empty a small can of tomatoes or baked beans, take the top and bottom off with a can opener, and wash well. There you have it, a home-made ring!

Slowly melt the chocolate in a bowl over a pan of simmering water until just melted (do not allow to get too hot).

Using a hand whisk, add the chestnut purée to the melted chocolate, and whisk until smooth. The mixture will be quite thick, so you may want to beat it with a wooden spoon as well. Whisk in the crème fraîche and icing sugar. Carefully beat in 2 tablespoons of the whipped cream, then fold in the rest until smooth.

Arrange eight cooking rings on a baking tray. Spoon in the mousse and leave to set in the fridge. You can also do this in ramekins or a glass bowl.

Remove the rings. Serve with fresh raspberries and a little pouring cream.

To cook in the Aga **Melt the chocolate gently in a bowl on the back of the Aga.**

Tip **If preparing the day before, you will need to line the metal rings with clingfilm so the metal doesn't affect the mousse. The chestnut purée can be bought in all good supermarkets. I use the unsweetened type in a can, as it is firmer and helps the mousse to set.**

White Chocolate Bliss

This dessert – creamy, richly sweet, with an interesting added texture – is perfect for that special dinner party as it's quick to make and can be prepared 24 hours ahead. Serve it with a puddle of raspberry coulis if you like (see secret page 157).

Serves 6 Preparation time 10 minutes: Not suitable for freezing

225 g (8 oz) good-quality white chocolate (Lindt), broken into pieces
450 ml (15 fl oz) double cream, lightly whipped

3 egg whites
75 g (3 oz) ratafia biscuits, coarsely crushed
75 g (3 oz) roasted hazelnuts (see Tip), coarsely chopped

You will need a 2.2 litre (4 pint) shallow pretty bowl or serving dish.

Carefully melt the chocolate in a bowl over a pan of gently simmering water, stirring occasionally (be careful not to let it get too hot or the chocolate will become grainy). Set aside to cool.

Pour the melted chocolate into the whipped cream and carefully mix. Whisk the egg whites until stiff and fold into the cream mixture.

Spoon half the cream mixture into the base of the bowl. Sprinkle over half the crushed biscuits and hazelnuts. Spoon over the remaining cream mixture, level the top and sprinkle over the remaining biscuits and nuts.

Chill for an hour or so, but serve at room temperature.

To cook in the Aga **Melt the chocolate in a bowl on the back of the Aga.**

Tip **It is important for the hazelnuts to be roasted as this gives a lovely depth of flavour. Ready-roasted hazelnuts can be bought in all good supermarkets. If you are unable to get them, buy chopped or whole hazelnuts and dry fry in a pan over a high heat until brown. You don't need any oil as the natural fat comes out of the nuts while browning. But do watch carefully as they burn very quickly.**

a secret from our kitchen

White chocolate can be tricky to use if it is overheated – it becomes grainy and refuses to thicken. Firstly use a good-quality chocolate, and gently heat, being sure not to let it get too hot. Cooling it a little before mixing with the cream prevents the heat from knocking the air out of the cream.

Chocolate Chip Trifle –
The Full Monty

This is a trendy trifle, using Bailey's instead of sherry – one for the girls! If you like chocolate chip ice-cream, you'll love this. Buy the thin chocolate mints – chocolate with tiny chunks of mint – and not the chocolates with the runny mint centre.

Serves 6 – or 1 if you eat nothing else all day! Preparation time 10 minutes:
Not suitable for freezing

8 trifle sponges
6 tablespoons Bailey's Irish Cream
1 x 400 g can pear halves in natural juice
300 ml (10 fl oz) double cream

1 x 250 g tub mascarpone cheese
200 g (8 oz) mint chocolate wafer thins
fresh mint, to garnish
icing sugar, to dust

You will need a shallow glass bowl of about 1.5 litre (2¾ pint) capacity.

Slice the trifle sponges horizontally through the middle. Use eight halves to cover the base of the glass bowl. Sprinkle over 3 tablespoons of the Bailey's and 2 tablespoons of juice from the can of pears.

Whisk together the cream and mascarpone in a large bowl until lightly whipped (be careful not to over-whisk). Reserve six of the chocolate thins and chop the rest so they are still very chunky – about the size of hazelnuts. Mix the chopped chocolate in with the cream.

Cut the pear halves into 1 cm (½ in) slices and lay over the soaked sponge mixture. Spread with half the cream mixture and repeat the whole process again starting with the sponge. Coarsely chop the remaining chocolate thins and sprinkle over the top.

Leave to chill in the fridge for a minimum of 2 hours, and serve garnished with fresh mint and a dusting of icing sugar.

Tip If you prefer, you could use brandy or rum instead of Bailey's. Remember to keep Bailey's in the fridge; because it has a cream base, it can easily go off (although I find it doesn't last long enough to worry about!).If you have over-whipped your cream and it looks a little curdled, add a little pouring cream and stir in (don't whisk) and the cream will become smooth again.

Old-fashioned Gooseberry Fool

This is a fool made in the classic way, but one that is lighter in fat because I have used a proportion of low-fat crème fraîche. It can also be made with other fruits when in season. I think it looks best served in cocktail or wine glasses.

Serves 4 Preparation time 10 minutes: Cooking time 10 minutes: Not suitable for freezing

900 g (2 lb) fresh gooseberries, topped and tailed

2 tablespoons elderflower cordial

100 g (4 oz) caster sugar

1 x 200 ml carton half-fat crème fraîche

300 ml (10 fl oz) double cream, lightly whipped

fresh elderflower or mint, to garnish

Measure the prepared fruit into a large saucepan with the elderflower cordial and sugar, and cover with a lid. Simmer over a low heat for about 10 minutes or until the gooseberries are soft, stirring occasionally.

Sieve the gooseberries over a large bowl so only the skin and seeds remain in the sieve (discard these). Carefully stir the crème fraîche into the gooseberry pulp, then fold in the whipped cream.

Spoon into four large wine glasses and chill (it will not set, but it will thicken up a little). Decorate with elderflower sprigs or mint, and serve chilled.

To cook in the Aga Cook the gooseberries, elderflower cordial and sugar, covered, in the simmering oven for about 10 minutes until soft.

Tip If you like texture, you do not need to sieve the gooseberries. I'm not keen on pips or skin, which is why I sieve them. If you don't have elderflower cordial, use apple juice or water instead.

---

a secret from our kitchen

Topping and tailing gooseberries in the summer always reminds me of Mary. Paul, Mary's lovely husband, picks the gooseberries and arrives in the kitchen with a large trug of fruit. Mary's heart sinks as she has to set to, and top and tail pounds of fruit ready for cooking or freezing. Many a recipe has been discussed and devised while preparing fruit at our desks!

Sunset Fruit Salad with Fresh Lime

The combination here of passionfruit and fresh lime is wonderful, and it is refreshing enough on its own, but some will prefer it with ice-cream or cream. I have made a sugar syrup, because I think it really makes all the difference to a fruit salad.

Serves 6 Preparation time 10 minutes: Not suitable for freezing

2 oranges
4 passionfruit
1 pineapple, peeled, cored and cut
    into 2.5 cm (1 in) chunks
1 ripe mango, peeled (see page 30)

Lime syrup
100 g (4 oz) caster sugar
150 ml (5 fl oz) water
juice and finely grated zest of 1 lime

a secret from our kitchen

During our demonstrations all our 'punters' taste the recipes we have made. This is the last recipe I do on one of our summer days, and even though everyone is pretty full, I insist they try this sauce because it is so refreshing and unusual. They all love it, and I hope you do too.

For the syrup, slowly dissolve the sugar in a saucepan with the water over a low heat, stirring. Once all the sugar has dissolved, bring to the boil. Boil rapidly over a high heat for about 5 minutes. Remove the pan from the heat and allow to cool. Add the lime zest and juice.

Peel and segment the oranges into a serving bowl, reserving the juice for later. Cut the passionfruit in half, scoop out the pulp and seeds and add to the oranges. Slice the mango flesh into thin 7.5 cm (3 in) long strips and mix with the other fruit.

Pour the lime syrup over the fruit, add any saved orange juice, and chill.

Tip I love this fruit salad all being one colour, but if you feel it needs more colour, you can, of course, add strawberries or raspberries as well.

Long Tall Sally Meringue with Mango and Passionfruit

a secret from our kitchen

Two of the most common readers' letters or e-mail queries we get are, 'Why do my meringues collapse?' and 'Why is there toffee coming out of the bottom of my meringue?' These problems are a result of the way the meringue has been made – they both occur when the sugar isn't incorporated well enough. If you whisk the mixture fast, adding the sugar slowly as outlined above, you won't have any further problems.

Mary calls me the 'queen of meringues', but it's only because she has taught me properly! The foolproof way of making meringues I give below really works. Meringues or pavlovas are usually round, but I like to make long thin ones. If you double this recipe, you will have four meringues which, arranged end to end on a foil platter, look stunning. I did this for a summer party a few years ago (see below!). It looks very impressive and, after a few drinks, everyone is quite confused as to how you managed to fit it into the oven!

Serves 8 Preparation time 10 minutes: Cooking time $1^{1}/_{2}$ – 2 hours: Not suitable for freezing

4 egg whites
225 g (8 oz) caster sugar
Topping
150 ml (5 fl oz) double cream
1 x 200g tub low-fat Greek yoghurt
4 passionfruit

1 large ripe mango, peeled and stoned, flesh cut into 1 cm ($^{1}/_{2}$ in) dice (see page 30)
100 g (4 oz) raspberries
fresh mint, to garnish
icing sugar, to dust

Preheat the oven to 120°C/250°F/Gas $^{1}/_{2}$. Line a large baking sheet with bakewell paper or non-stick silicone paper.

Whisk the egg whites with an electric hand whisk in a large clean bowl until they are as stiff as they can get. Still whisking on maximum speed (move the whisk around the bowl), gradually add the sugar a teaspoon at a time until all the sugar is incorporated and it is shiny and the meringue holds in stiff peaks (this whole process will take about 8–10 minutes). Whisk in between each addition of sugar on maximum speed, which keeps the sugar suspended in the egg white. (The meringue can also be made in a free-standing mixer.)

Spread the meringue into two long thin rectangles of about 43 x 15 cm

(17 x 6 in), with a gap between the two as the meringues may spread a little. Bake in the preheated oven for about 1½–2 hours or until the meringue can be lifted easily from the paper without sticking. Turn off the oven, leave the door ajar and leave the meringues until cold.

Whip the cream to soft peaks in a large bowl, then stir in the yoghurt. Halve the passionfruit and scoop out the pips and juice into the cream mixture. Stir in the mango pieces, and mix together.

Arrange the meringues end to end on a platter or a foil-covered piece of wood. Spoon on the cream mixture and scatter the raspberries over the top. Garnish with fresh mint and dust with icing sugar.

To cook in the Aga Slide the baking sheet into the simmering oven for about 1½– 2 hours until the meringue is crisp and can be easily lifted from the paper.

Tip Meringues can be kept wrapped in clingfilm and foil for up to a month. If kept for a long period, they can become a little brittle, so, when using, assemble the meringue (with the fruit and cream) about 5 hours ahead, which will soften the meringue and make it perfect for eating. To enhance the cream's flavour, the passionfruit pips and juice can be added to the cream up to 24 hours ahead and then whipped (this will also soften the pips slightly).

Honeycomb Ice-cream with Bailey's

This ice-cream does not need an ice-cream maker or re-whizzing in a processor – just make it, freeze it and remove from the freezer 10 minutes before serving. It's a bit of a cheat, perhaps, using Crunchie bars, but it's so delicious. If you don't like the idea of using the booze, you can leave it out. This does contain raw egg yolks, so it shouldn't be served to those who are pregnant or elderly.

Serves about 8–12 Preparation time 15 minutes: Freezing time minimum 12 hours

3 eggs, separated
175 g (6 oz) caster sugar
300 ml (10 fl oz) double cream
3 large Crunchie bars, crushed into pieces
   about the size of almonds
3 tablespoons runny honey

To serve
about 6 tablespoons Bailey's Irish Cream

You will need a 1 litre (1³/₄ pint) plastic container with a lid, or 12 ramekins.

Beat the egg whites in a large bowl, using an electric hand mixer on maximum speed, until they are as stiff as they can get. Still on maximum speed, gradually add the sugar a little at a time to make a stiff shiny raw meringue mixture. Whisk the cream until it is just thick enough to hold its shape, then stir in the egg yolks. Stir the broken Crunchie bars and honey into the meringue mixture, and cut and fold the cream into it as well.

Spoon the mixture into ramekins or a plastic container. Cover and freeze for a minimum of 12 hours.

Remove the container(s) from the freezer about 10 minutes before serving, just to soften it a little, which will make it easier to scoop. Scoop the ice-cream into individual bowls and pour over a little Bailey's.

Tip Ice-cream is such a versatile dessert. You can make a basic ice-cream following the recipe above (omit the Crunchies and honey), and then add your own flavours. You could add the juice and finely grated rind of 2 lemons and limes, or 75 g (3 oz) chocolate chips and 2 teaspoons vanilla extract, or 2 tablespoons lemon or orange curd. There are so many variations.

a secret from our kitchen

When we filmed the *Mary Berry at Home* series for the BBC, all the final shots were taken in the garden in the height of summer. One recipe for an ice-cream bombe was very hard to get right, as the sun was streaming down and the ice-cream was melting. We got there in the end, but it was touch and go whether it was going to be ice-cream soup – hence no ice-cream photo in this book!

Coconut Lime Creams

These are very quick, but they are fairly rich, so I have made them quite small. They're perfect for a large dinner party as they are served cold. Be careful not to overcook as bubbles will appear and they will taste curdled: they should be smooth and melt in your mouth. Serve with the Sunset Fruit Salad on page 165 or the Honey-glazed Pineapple on page 149.

Serves 6 Preparation time 10 minutes: Cooking time 25 minutes: Not suitable for freezing

butter for greasing
1 lime
2 x 200 ml cartons coconut cream
150 ml (5 fl oz) double cream

3 egg yolks
1 egg
100 g (4 oz) caster sugar

Preheat the oven to 160°C/325°F/Gas 3. Butter six timbale moulds or size 1 ramekins, and sit in a small roasting tin. Finely grate the zest from the lime, then peel and segment the lime.

Measure the coconut cream, double cream and lime zest into a saucepan, and bring to simmering point, but do not allow to boil.

Whisk the egg yolks, egg and caster sugar together in a bowl until combined. Pour in the hot cream and whisk until well blended.

Divide the mixture evenly between the timbale moulds. Pour boiling water into the roasting tin until it comes halfway up the sides of the moulds (this is a bain-marie). Bake in the preheated oven for about 20–25 minutes until just set but still with a slight wobble. Set aside to cool.

Dip the moulds in hot water (to help the creams come out) and turn on to plates. Decorate with fresh mint and lime segments.

To cook in the Aga Slide the bain-marie on to the lowest set of runners in the roasting oven for about 5–8 minutes (do not let the creams bubble or go brown). Transfer to the simmering oven for about 25–30 minutes until just set. Set aside to cool.

Tip Coconut cream is UHT and comes in cartons that are available in all good supermarkets in the Indian/Thai section. Do not use coconut milk, as the creams will not set firm enough to turn out. We have also made these as orange and lemon creams. Omit the lime and replace with the grated zest of a lemon or orange. Omit the coconut cream, and replace with a further 400 ml (14 fl oz) double cream.

time for tea

Auntie Jill's Chocolate and Orange Cake

As a child I would go with my family to visit Auntie Jill in Wiltshire. I remember the smell of baking as if it were yesterday, and on special days the wonderful smell of yeast when she made Chelsea buns. This Auntie Jill cake is so moist because of the evaporated milk. I have changed the recipe slightly and added orange zest, and I can assure you everyone will love it.

Serves 6 Preparation time 10 minutes: Cooking time 20 minutes:
Freezes well, cakes separately, un-iced

50 g (2 oz) cocoa powder
5 tablespoons boiling water
3 eggs
1 x 175 g can evaporated milk
175 g (6 oz) self-raising flour
1 level teaspoon baking powder
225 g (8 oz) caster sugar
100 g (4 oz) margarine (see Tip)
finely grated zest of 1 small orange
50 g (2 oz) shelled walnuts, chopped

Icing
remaining evaporated milk from the can
225 g (8 oz) orange-flavoured chocolate,
    eg Terry's or Lindt, broken into pieces
50 g (2 oz) shelled walnuts, chopped
icing sugar, sieved, to decorate

Preheat the oven to 160°C/325°F/Gas 3. Grease and base-line two 20 cm (8 in) cake tins.

Sieve the cocoa powder into a large mixing bowl and blend with the boiling water to make a smooth paste. In a separate bowl, beat together the eggs with 5 tablespoons evaporated milk from the can. Pour on to the cocoa, add the remaining ingredients and mix with an electric hand whisk until smooth. This can be done in a processor if preferred.

Divide the mixture between the two tins and spread out evenly to the sides. Bake in the preheated oven for about 15–20 minutes until the cakes begin to shrink from the sides of the tins and the tops spring back when pressed lightly. Turn out on to wire rack to cool.

To make the icing, pour the remaining evaporated milk from the can into a saucepan with the broken-up pieces of orange chocolate, and melt over a low heat until smooth and shiny. Cool slightly so that it thickens a little.

Spread one cake with 3 tablespoons of icing and sandwich the remaining cake on top. Spread the remaining icing on top and arrange the walnuts on the icing. Dust with sieved icing sugar once the icing has set.

To cook in the Aga Slide the cakes on to the grid shelf on the floor of the roasting oven and slide the cold sheet on the second set of runners. Bake for about 15–20 minutes until the cakes shrink away from the sides of the tins and the tops spring back if lightly pressed.

Tip If you do not like orange, leave it out and use Bournville chocolate for the icing. When making cakes in a processor, be careful not to over-beat, as this will make a dense cake, which will not rise so well. The fats you can buy in supermarkets have now changed. No longer can you buy Blue Band or Stork SB, which were margarines in tubs. What you now find in tubs are actually spreads, which have less fat and more water, therefore change the texture of the cake and make it close-textured and not light and fluffy. Make sure you use margarine (a high fat content) or softened butter.

Hummingbird Cake

This recipe is based on a good carrot cake, but instead of bananas (which are common in carrot cakes), I have used crushed pineapple. It is a very large cake – deep, high and delicious – which is wonderful for Sunday afternoon tea, or any time!

Serves 8 at least Preparation time 10 minutes: Cooking time 40 minutes: Freezes well un-iced

4 eggs
300 ml (10 fl oz) sunflower oil
225 g (8 oz) carrots, peeled and coarsely grated
1 x 227 g can crushed pineapple, drained well
450 g (1 lb) self-raising flour
300 g (10 oz) caster sugar

4 level teaspoons baking powder
1 teaspoon vanilla extract
100 g (4 oz) shelled walnuts, chopped, half for the cake, half for garnish

Icing
225 g (8 oz) rich cream cheese
175 g (6 oz) icing sugar, sieved
1 teaspoon vanilla extract

Preheat the oven to 180°C/350°F/Gas 4. Grease and base-line two 20 cm (8 in) deep cake tins.

Beat the eggs in a large mixing bowl to break them up. Add the oil, grated carrot and pineapple, and mix together with a wooden spoon. Stir in the remaining ingredients, including half the walnuts, and beat well until everything is incorporated. It is a very thick mixture.

Pour into the prepared cake tins and bake in the preheated oven for about 40 minutes until golden brown, firm to the touch and shrinking away from the sides of the tins. Set aside to cool. Turn out on to a wire rack to cool completely.

To make the icing, mix the cream cheese with the sieved icing sugar and vanilla in a bowl until smooth. Spoon a third of the mixture on to one cooled cake and sandwich the other one on top. Spread the remaining icing on top of the cake. Sprinkle with the remaining walnuts.

To cook in the Aga Slide the cake tins on to the grid shelf on the floor of the roasting oven with the cold sheet on the second set of runners for about 20 minutes until golden brown and set around the edges. Transfer the hot cold sheet to the simmering oven, put the cake tins on top and bake for further 40 minutes or until firm in the middle and shrinking away from the sides of the tins.

Tip Because this cake is very deep, it cuts even better the day after making. It tends to crumble a little if cut when too fresh.

Banana and Cinnamon Muffins

These are breakfast-style muffins, so are not very sweet. Actually, I think they are good at any time – with a cup of coffee, reading the paper on a Sunday morning or as a snack in the afternoon . . .

Makes 12 muffins Preparation time 10 minutes: Cooking time about 20 minutes:
Freeze well in a plastic bag

225 g (8 oz) self-raising flour, sieved
100 g (4 oz) light muscovado sugar
1½ teaspoons ground cinnamon
1 rounded teaspoon baking powder
1 ripe banana, peeled and mashed

125 ml (4 fl oz) milk
2 eggs, beaten
50 g (2 oz) butter, melted

Preheat the oven to 200°C/400°F/Gas 6. Grease 12 non-stick muffin tins, or line the tins with paper bun cases.

Measure the flour, sugar, cinnamon and baking powder into a large bowl. In a separate bowl, mix the banana, milk and eggs together until smooth. Pour the wet mixture into the dry mixture with the melted butter, and mix together with a wooden spoon until completely smooth. Spoon evenly into the muffin tins.

Bake in the preheated oven for about 15 minutes or until well risen and golden brown. Serve cold or, even nicer, just warmed.

To cook in the Aga Slide the muffin tray on to the grid shelf on the floor of the roasting oven with the cold sheet on the second set of runners for about 15–20 minutes or until well risen and golden brown.

Tip I have used light muscovado sugar in this recipe, which is a natural unrefined, soft brown sugar. It gives a richer, caramelised flavour, and also gives the muffins a golden brown colour. You can use caster sugar if preferred, but do not use granulated as it is too coarse and will give a speckled effect. Like all cakes that are low in fat they don't keep very well for long, so it's best to store them in the fridge. It's even better to freeze them. Thaw for 3 hours, then reheat for about 5 minutes in a moderate oven and serve warm.

Golden Flapjacks

I think the flapjack has been forgotten by most of us, but it is one of the easiest biscuits to make. Usually flapjacks come in squares, but instead of buying a special tin, I have made them in a round cake tin, as most of us have one of these.

Makes 16 flapjacks Preparation time 5 minutes: Cooking time 25 minutes: Freeze well cooked

a secret from our kitchen

It is tricky to weigh golden syrup and remove it from the scale pan, so this is our solution. Weigh the sugar first and then the syrup on top of the sugar, and then the syrup-topped sugar will slide out of the pan easily.

100 g (4 oz) butter

100 g (4 oz) demerara sugar

100 g (4 oz) golden syrup

225 g (8 oz) porridge oats (rolled oats)

Preheat the oven to 160°C/325°F/Gas 3. Grease and base-line a 20 cm (8 in) round cake tin.

Measure the butter, sugar and syrup into a saucepan. Heat gently over a low heat, stirring, until the butter has melted and the sugar has dissolved. Remove the pan from the heat, and stir in the oats. Pour into the lined tin, and press down with the back of a spoon until the surface is level.

Bake in the preheated oven for about 25–30 minutes until golden brown. Remove from the oven, loosen from the sides of the tin with a palette knife, and leave to cool for about 10 minutes.

Tip out on to a board, remove the paper, and cut into 16 even-sized wedges (or whichever size you like). Leave to cool completely.

To cook in the Aga Slide the tin on to the grid shelf on the floor of the roasting oven with the cold sheet on the second set of runners for about 10–12 minutes or until golden brown.

Tip The best oats to use are breakfast porridge oats, i.e. rolled oats. Avoid jumbo oats as they are too large for these flapjacks.

Apple and Sultana Scotch Pancakes

These are delicious as a dessert, spread with lemon curd for tea – or even for breakfast with butter on. When testing the recipe, instead of a bowl of soup for lunch, I had two pancakes with a banana, vanilla ice-cream and maple syrup – very naughty but very delicious! The pancakes are a little thicker than drop scones or plain Scotch pancakes; because of the apples, they should not be too thin.

a secret from our kitchen

I was taught always to leave a pancake or Yorkshire pudding batter to stand before using, to allow the starch cells to swell and any tiny lumps to disperse. Now I make my batter using an electric hand whisk, which gives a smooth result, with no lumps in sight, and it can therefore be cooked straightaway.

Makes about 12 pancakes Preparation time 10 minutes: Cooking time about 15 minutes: Freeze very well when cooked

25 g (1 oz) butter
225 g (8 oz) dessert apples, peeled, cored and finely chopped
25 g (1 oz) sultanas
a little sunflower oil

Batter
225 g (8 oz) self-raising flour
1 teaspoon baking powder
50 g (2 oz) caster sugar
2 eggs, beaten
150 ml (5 fl oz) milk

Heat the butter in a small pan, add the apples and cook over a low heat for about 5 minutes until the apples are softened, but not a mush. Stir in the sultanas and leave to cool.

For the batter, mix the flour, baking powder and sugar in a bowl. Make a well in the centre, add the eggs and gradually whisk in the milk to make a smooth batter. Stir in the cooled apples and sultanas.

Heat a little oil in non-stick frying pan, just enough to coat the pan. Spoon in a generous tablespoon of batter, allowing it to spread slightly. Cook for about 2–3 minutes until bubbles appear in the batter, then flip over and cook for a further 2–3 minutes until golden brown. Set aside whilst making the remaining pancakes. Keep warm.

To cook in the Aga Lift the lid of the simmering plate for about 5 minutes to cool it a little. Using a piece of kitchen towel, grease the simmering plate. Spoon a generous tablespoon of batter directly on to the simmering plate for about 2 minutes until bubbles start to appear in the batter. Flip over and cook for a further 2 minutes on the other side. Repeat using the rest of the batter. Keep warm in the simmering oven.

Indulgent Chocolate Brownies

These are just too delicious to refuse. I put on about half a stone testing this recipe to get it perfect! I have added chocolate chips to give extra chocolatiness.

Makes about 20 pieces Preparation time 15 minutes: Cooking time 45 minutes: Freeze well

350 g (12 oz) Bournville chocolate, broken into pieces

225 g (8 oz) unsalted butter, cut into pieces

4 eggs

225 g (8 oz) light muscovado sugar

1 teaspoon vanilla extract

75 g (3 oz) self-raising flour

100 g (4 oz) dark chocolate chips

Preheat the oven to 190°C/375°F/Gas 5. Grease and line a traybake tin or small roasting tin about 30 x 33 cm (12 x 9 in) with foil.

Melt the chocolate and butter together in a bowl set over a pan of gently simmering water until smooth and completely melted (do not allow to get too hot).

Using a wooden spoon, beat the eggs, sugar and vanilla in a large bowl. Pour in the melted chocolate and butter and stir. Stir in the flour and chocolate chips and beat until smooth.

Pour into the prepared tin and bake in the preheated oven for about 40–45 minutes or until firm to the touch and a light crust has formed on top. Leave to cool in the tin before cutting into pieces.

To cook in the Aga Slide the tin on to the grid shelf on the floor of the roasting oven with the cold sheet on the second set of runners for about 20 minutes until fairly firm and a light crust has formed on the top. Transfer the hot cold sheet to the simmering oven, slide the tin on top and continue to bake for a further 20 minutes until firm and shrinking away from the sides of the tin.

Tip Brownies, like gingerbread, are likely to dip a little in the middle. This is correct and means they are nice and gooey inside, as they should be. Don't be tempted to overcook or they will become dry.

a secret from our kitchen

The easiest way to line a roasting tin with foil is to turn the tin upside down, mould the foil over the top, turn the tin back over and the foil case will drop into the tin. This is a special Mary tip!

Fruit Loaf with Fresh Lime and Ginger

This is a refreshingly light fruit cake with a lovely lime icing. The recipe fills two 450 g (1 lb) loaf tins, so make both of them in one go, eat one and freeze the other un-iced. (It is always better to ice a cake on the day of eating.)

Makes 2 loaves Preparation time 10 minutes: Cooking time 45 minutes:
Freezes well, cakes separate, un-iced

175 g (6 oz) self-raising flour
100 g (4 oz) margarine (see the Tip on page 173)
100 g (4 oz) caster sugar
3 eggs, beaten
50 g (2 oz) raisins
50 g (2 oz) glacé cherries, quartered, washed and dried well

150 g (5 oz) sultanas
4 bulbs stem ginger, finely chopped
finely grated zest of 2 limes

Icing
100 g (4 oz) icing sugar, sieved
2 tablespoons lime juice
1 bulb stem ginger, chopped
finely grated zest of 1 small lime

Preheat the oven to 160°C/325°F/Gas 3. Grease and base-line two 450 g (1 lb) loaf tins.

Measure all the ingredients for the cakes into a large bowl. Mix well until smooth. Divide evenly between the two loaf tins, and level the tops.

Bake in the preheated oven for about 45–50 minutes until golden brown. To test if cooked, insert a skewer into the middle the cake; if it comes out clean, the cake is cooked. Leave to cool in the tins.

When cold, remove the cakes from the tins and make the icing. Mix the icing sugar and lime juice together in a bowl until smooth. Spread over the top of the cakes. Garnish with ginger down the centre and arrange lime zest over the top.

To cook in the Aga Slide the loaf tins on to the grid shelf on the floor of the roasting oven with the cold sheet on the second set of runners for about 15–20 minutes until golden brown. Transfer the hot cold sheet to the simmering oven, put the loaves on top and bake for a further 20 minutes until set and cooked through. Test with a skewer as above.

Tip The easiest way to line a loaf tin is to cut one piece of baking parchment to fit across the wide sides of the tin only, from one edge down over the base and up to the other edge. Don't worry about lining the ends of the tin.

Another of our commonest letters or e-mails from readers asks, 'Why does the fruit sink to the bottom of a fruit or cherry cake?' This will only happen if the cake mix is too soft, over-beaten, or if the fruit is too wet or syrupy. That is why it is so important here to wash the syrup off the glacé cherries and to dry them really well. A cake such as a Christmas cake will be fine, as it is more packed with fruit, for the more fruit the cake has, the harder it is for the fruit to sink!

Tiramisù Traybake
with Pecans

In my opinion traybakes are the easiest cakes of all to make, especially when trying to feed a lot of people. They are perfect for packed lunches, or for selling at sales and bazaars. They do not require a special tin, as most of us have a small roasting tin that can be lined with foil.

Makes 21 pieces Preparation time 10 minutes: Cooking time 40 minutes: Freezes well un-iced

225 g (8 oz) soft butter or margarine
225 g (8 oz) caster sugar
300 g (10 oz) self-raising flour
2 level teaspoons baking powder
4 eggs
4 tablespoons milk
3 teaspoons instant coffee, dissolved in
    1 tablespoon boiling water
50 g (2 oz) shelled pecan nuts, chopped

Icing and topping
225 g (8 oz) icing sugar
2 teaspoons instant coffee, dissolved in
    $2^1/_2$ tablespoons boiling water
cocoa powder, to dust

a secret from our kitchen

It is important to weigh baking powder correctly, ideally with a measuring spoon. Don't be tempted to add a little extra powder, thinking it will help your cake to rise. Your cake will in fact rise up in the oven, but once it comes out it will fall again and have a dip in the middle, so always follow the recipe accurately.

Preheat the oven to 180°C/350°F/Gas 4. Grease and line a 30 x 23 cm (12 x 9 in) traybake tin with foil.

Measure all the cake ingredients, apart from the nuts, into a large mixing bowl. Mix together using an electric hand whisk until smooth and well blended. Stir in the nuts.

Pour the mixture into the lined tin and level the top. Bake in the preheated oven for about 35–40 minutes or until dark golden brown and shrinking away from the edges of the tin. Leave to cool for 10 minutes in the tin, then turn out on to a wire rack.

For the icing, sieve the icing sugar into a mixing bowl. Pour in the coffee, and blend together until smooth. Pour on top of the cooled cake and spread out to the edges. Leave to set, then dust with sieved cocoa powder. Cut into squares.

To cook in the Aga Slide the tin on to the grid shelf on the floor of the roasting oven with the cold sheet on the second set of runners for about 30–35 minutes, changing the cold sheet after 20 minutes if it begins to get too brown.

Tip If preferred, use walnuts instead of pecans.

Strawberry and Banana Smoothie

Smoothies are perfect at any time of day. They are not as sweet as milkshakes, but if you would like yours sweeter just add a little more icing sugar to the recipe below. Alternatively, to make a milkshake, add some vanilla ice-cream.

Serves 2–6 Preparation time and making time 5 mins: Not suitable for freezing

1 just ripe medium banana
350 g (12 oz) ripe strawberries
150 ml (¼ pint) single cream

300 ml (½ pint) milk
2 tablespoons icing sugar
few mint leaves for garnish

Measure all the ingredients into a processor and whiz until smooth. (You can also whiz this with a hand-held mixer in a bowl if preferred).

Serve cold with a few fresh mint leaves floating on the top.

Tip Smoothies are best served chilled. They can be made up to 3 hours ahead (but no longer than this as the banana will discolour). I use icing sugar for this recipe as it dissolves in the liquid – if you only have caster sugar you can use it instead, the difference is, it will give a slightly grainy texture.

a secret from our kitchen

I often use strawberries as a garnish for desserts for our workshops or for food photography for Mary's books. I always leave the top green leaves on and cut through the stem: it looks so much more attractive this way.

Home-made
stocks

Poultry or Game Stock

Pack the cooked or raw bones (never mix cooked and raw) tightly in a saucepan, and add the flavouring vegetables, herbs and spices (see opposite). Just cover with water, bring to the boil, cover and simmer for between 1 and 4 hours until it is a golden brown colour. Sieve, cool and store in plastic pots.

Beef Stock

Always use raw beef bones and brown them ahead by roasting in a moderate oven for about 15 minutes. This gives both a deeper flavour and a brown colour to the stock. Pack the bones tightly into a saucepan, add flavouring vegetables, herbs and spices (see opposite), just cover with water, bring to the boil, cover and simmer for 3–4 hours. Sieve, cool and store in plastic pots.

Vegetable Stock

Use well flavoured vegetables, but not starchy ones such as potatoes and parsnips. Cut the vegetables into chunks – carrots, onions, celery, spring onion whites – then add extra flavourings – a bay leaf, some black peppercorns, parsley stalks, onion skins. Pack them tightly in a saucepan and just cover with water. Bring to the boil, cover and simmer for 1–2 hours until well flavoured. Sieve, cool and store in plastic cartons.

Home-made stocks can make the all the difference to a recipe, but there are
a few general rules.

- Never mix raw bones and cooked bones when making stock. They are best
  used separately.
- Add flavourings such as onion, celery, carrots, parsley stalks, a bay leaf and
  a few black peppercorns. Cut the onion into chunks. Don't use starchy
  vegetables such as potatoes as they make the stock cloudy, or strongly
  flavoured root vegetables such as swede and parsnip. Green vegetables make
  the stock slimy.
- Add onion skins to the liquid, as these give a lovely colour to your stock.
- You cannot buy bones from supermarkets any more but you can from your
  local butcher. Order ahead and, if you are a regular customer, it is likely
  they will be very reasonably priced.
- For beef stock, ask the butcher to saw large bones into manageable pieces so
  they will fit easily into a saucepan. Brown ahead by roasting and just cover
  with water, this will give a more intensely flavoured stock. The perfect stock
  will become a jelly when cool.
- For large chicken bones – a chicken carcass, for instance – freeze in two
  large poly bags, bash with a wooden rolling pin and they will break up
  easily.
- Always sieve a stock just in case there are small splinters of bones.
- Season with salt and pepper, but don't overdo it; bear in mind that you will
  be seasoning the dish as well.
- For a really intensely flavoured stock you can reduce it so it is very dark
  brown and reduced in volume.
- To freeze stock, pour into plastic pots and set aside to cool. Any fat from the
  stock will rise to the top and act as a seal, therefore you will not need a lid.
  When using for a recipe, remove any fat from the top before adding to the
  dish. If liked, use the fat for the roux.
- Pheasant and other game bird stock is wonderful and full of flavour, ideal for
  game casseroles or pies.
- To cook stock in the Aga, bring the stock to the boil on the boiling plate,
  cover and transfer to the simmering oven for 2–6 hours, or overnight (for
  beef stock).

It's all in a day's work ...

Feeling peckish!

Mary and I at the kitchen table,
planning a workshop.

*An Aga's not just a cooker – our favourite
place to relax after a day of demonstration*

*In the office
contemplating the
start of another
busy week.*

It's all for me at the Christmas party!

*Lucinda and me laughing at
another of Mary's jokes.*

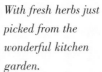

With fresh herbs just picked from the wonderful kitchen garden.

Coco won't come in again.

In the glasshouse by the vines, but where have all the grapes gone?

Mary's favourite gardening tip – dig then pull. Leeks, that is!

Two Father Christmas impersonators. Where's Rudolf? In the Aga!

187

Workshop information

Mary Berry website – information on Aga Workshops and
Mary Berry & Daughter Ltd (Salad Dressings and Sauces)
www.maryberry.co.uk

Lakeland Ltd – Kitchen equipment suppliers
Alexander Buildings
Windermere
Cumbria
LA23 1BQ
Tel 01539 488100
www.lakelandlimited.co.uk

Aga Rayburn
Station Road
Ketley
Telford
Shropshire
TF15AQ
Tel 01952 642000 Head Office
Tel 0845 6023015 Aga Servicing and Technical Enquiries
www.aga-rayburn.co.uk
www.agalinks.co.uk
www.agacookshop.co.uk

ICTC – kitchen suppliers
3 Caley Close
Sweet Briar Rd
Norwich
Norfolk
NR32BU
Tel 01603 488019
www.ictc.co.uk

Acknowledgements

Firstly, I should like to thank my best friend and mentor, Mary Berry. Mary has thanked me so many times in her books, now it is my turn! Without Mary, I doubt very much whether I would have had the chance to write this book. She has taught me all that I know about writing, and I am so lucky to be in a job which I love and where I continue to learn. There is no better teacher than Mary: she has encouraged me, given me faith and confidence, and pushed me further than I thought I could be pushed! She is generous with her time and expertise, and I am truly grateful to her and her family for welcoming me as one of them.

Secondly, I should like to say a huge thank you to Lucinda Kaizak, who works with me at Mary's. Lucinda trained at Leith's and joined us as our student for a year; she turned out to be a gem, so we didn't let her go, and she is still with us four years later! She has helped me with the testing of the recipes and continually said how excited she was to be involved, which has meant a lot. We have shared ideas and laughed along the way. Thank you, Lucinda, for keeping me sane when the deadline was getting closer!

Thank you to Carey Smith at Ebury Press for the phone call 18 months ago asking if I would like to write a book. It's been a pleasure working with you, Carey, and I'm grateful for your belief in me. Thank you too to Philip Webb for the stunning photos in this book. Philip came for a week's shoot, and I am thrilled with his work and his passion for the finest detail. Susan Fleming, my editor, has gone through every recipe in great detail – thank you so much for all your hard work. Thank you too to my agent (I've always wanted to say that!), Michelle Topham at Felicity Bryan, for taking me on. It is lovely to know you are at the end of the phone.

Finally, I should like to thank my very lovely friends, especially Robbie Woolford, who helped with the typing, managing to read my writing and understand all my scruffy notes. Last but not least, I want to thank my family: my wonderful parents for supporting me the whole way, even when I didn't quite think I could get through it all; my three lovely brothers for their humour and teasing; and my three gorgeous sisters-in law. Thanks to all of you for tasting and being honest.

And I must thank you for buying the book. I hope you have as much fun cooking and eating the recipes as I have had creating them.

Index